A Taxonomy of Office Chairs

A Taxonomy of Office Chairs

The evolution of the office chair, demonstrated through a catalogue of seminal models and an illustrated taxonomy of their components

Jonathan Olivares

Our urban civilization is witness to an ever-accelerating procession of generations of products, appliances and gadgets by comparison with which mankind appears to be a remarkably stable species. This pullulation of objects is no odder, when we come to think about it, than that to be observed in countless natural species. Species which man has successfully inventoried.

...everyday objects proliferate, needs multiply, production speeds up the life-span of such objects – yet we lack the vocabulary to name them all. How can we hope to classify a world of objects that changes before our very eyes and arrive at an adequate system of description?

– Jean Baudrillard, *The System of Objects*

Contents

Foreword

From an 1849 metal and wood 'business' chair to the engineered fabrics, polymer fibres and intuitive mechanisms of twenty-first century ergonomic seating, *A Taxonomy of Office Chairs* by Jonathan Olivares documents the major inventions, innovations and technology that have shaped the evolution of office chairs. When introduced to Jonathan several years ago by Stefano Boeri, then editor of *Domus* for whom Jonathan was writing a piece on American furniture manufacturers, I was impressed by the intelligence and curiosity of this recent Pratt Institute grad. As director of design at Knoll I saw an opportunity to pursue the company's commitment to support young designers while also contributing to the store of history and research that are the foundation for what we do. Knoll funded Jonathan's research and helped arrange meetings with designers, furniture manufacturers, and other experts in order to facilitate his work on what we knew would be a valuable reference book.

This book is important because it covers ground that has never before been documented in a systematic way. The taxonomic approach provides neutral, independent information without judgements, aesthetic or otherwise. And the subject matter is of critical interest because of the major role that the office chair has played not only in the evolution of how we sit to work, but of work itself. *A Taxonomy of Office Chairs* helps us understand both the historical and the anthropological context of work in the office-place and its relation to the objects that make it possible. Thank you, Jonathan, for your fine work. It has been my pleasure to help facilitate the process.

Benjamin A. Pardo

Illustrations from *Hortus Cliffortianus*, an early work of taxonomic literature
Carolus Linnaeus, Amsterdam, 1737

Preface

As far as I am aware, this book is the first taxonomy of an industrialized object. I find it ironic and unnerving that our society cherishes, studies and documents the natural world, but keeps little track of the products that make up our predominant reality. The books found in the design sections of our libraries and bookstores, biased by taste and personal approach, focus almost exclusively on best-case-scenario products – all lovely things unless you are trying to get an objective analysis of a product's evolution over a long period of time. This book could have been the taxonomy of toasters or automotive engines, but office chairs seemed an ideal subject because of their close relationship with the human body and their mechanical complexity. The aim of this book is to provide an objective source on the structural, morphological, material, and mechanical development of the office chair and its various components, and to contextualize these mutations culturally and in relation to each other.

The book is divided into four main sections. The first is an essay on the history of office chairs that addresses the larger social and industrial shifts that swayed office chair design. The second is a catalogue of chairs with images and brief descriptions of all of the chairs featured, with emphasis placed on chairs that significantly altered the course of office chair design. The third section is the taxonomy itself, and is divided into chapters that explain the evolution of the various parts of chairs with illustrations and descriptions. In these chapters, all the variations of each component are explained and chronicled. For instance, the backrest chapter reviews backrests held by single, double or multiple spines separately, and shows the evolution of each. The final section of the book highlights the methods of movement that have reinvented the way in which office chairs move and support the body. The last three sections of the book cross-reference each other. Page numbers, which are listed by each chair, component and movement type, allow the reader to navigate back and forth through the sections.

During the first phase of our research we gathered as many office chairs as we could find and naively attempted to organize some 2,000 of them into a massive family tree. We arranged images of chairs chronologically along a wall, using black tape to connect chairs that had similar features. We began to see the history of the armrest, the backrest and the base, but the resulting cobweb of black lines was illegible. We understood that to coherently map the evolution of the office chair, we would have to study each component separately.

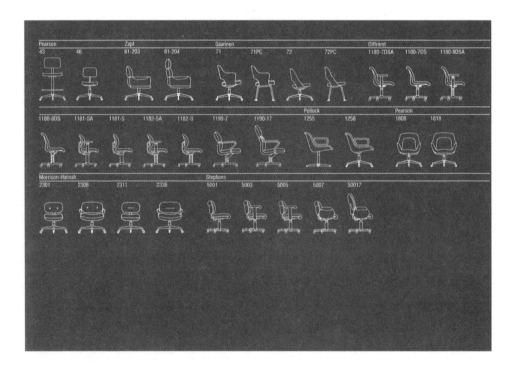

Knoll catalogue, 1980

We decided that chairs would only be included in the book if they were the first to introduce a given feature. Unlike plants and animals that evolve slowly over thousands of years, products are subject to frequent and spontaneous mutations at the hands of their designers. For this reason, I made it a priority to find the first instances of given features, place them historically and credit their inventors.

To find the first instance of a given feature you must survey all the available office chairs, organized chronologically, and locate what you believe to be the original. This information must then be verified or disproved with archival catalogues and books, interviews with designers, engineers, and museum curators, or encounters with actual chairs. It took two years of interviewing designers and engineers before I found someone who knew the origin of the height-adjustable armrest. He was certain that it was a version of Jørgen Rasmussen's Kevi chair, but I'm still not 100 percent sure that he was right.

Working with furniture manufacturers to uncover information was a challenging process. Most manufacturers discard their old catalogues, and when a company is purchased or goes out of business its records are usually the first thing to disappear after its knowledgeable employees. Out of the 100 or so manufacturers I contacted, only two had a professional archivist on staff.

Nevertheless, the manufacturers we spoke with happily provided all the information they had, and made valuable introductions to industry veterans, who are the most knowledgeable individuals when it comes to office chairs. There are probably fewer than 100 of these characters in the world, and to meet and interview thirty of them took the better part of two years and a healthy travel budget. The late Egon Bräuning, lead engineer at Vitra for forty years until his death in 2009, had an incredible wealth of information and eagerly shared it. Kurt Heidmann, a career-long engineer at Steelcase, was able to recall the first pneumatic cylinders used to adjust a chair's height. A Taxonomy of Office Chairs is largely an oral history, which my collaborators and I have transcribed.

Physical access to chairs made before 1970 often requires a visit to a design museum or its archive. Die Neue Sammlung in Munich, The Victoria and Albert Museum in London and the Vitra Design Museum in Weil am Rhein, Germany, are incredible resources on the most prized office chairs ever designed. Visits to these museums and their archives allowed me to study and photograph every detail of some of the best chairs designed before 1970. Finding a good photograph of the underside of an office chair – which is where all the action happens – is extremely difficult, so the chance to take them myself was invaluable.

One of the most exciting and rewarding aspects of making this book was interviewing many of the designers whose chairs are featured. If visiting them was possible, I jumped at the chance, because the designer of a chair always understands it best and meeting him or her in person can be a transformative and entertaining experience. The highlights of these encounters could easily be a book in itself, so a quick summary will have to suffice: Richard Sapper explained how he first put the steel car-bumper industry out of business by inventing the plastic bumper for Fiat in the 1970s, and then saved those companies by designing the Sapper chair for Knoll, which uses the same steel-rolling technology. Don Chadwick conveyed the risky process of designing the Aeron Chair with Bill Stumpf. Mario Bellini told me that the three greatest events in office chair history were, the Industrial Revolution, his 1984 Persona chair because it re-introduced humanism to office seating, and his 2005 Headline chair because it re-established the connection between man and desk. Other highlights were a tour of the basement of Studio 7.5, which is filled with hundreds of welded and thermoformed prototypes of the office chairs they have designed, and the walk through Niels Diffrient's barn-office in Ridgefield, Connecticut where he showed me the chairs he has designed over the last four decades. And finally, a trip to the little town of Hildesheim, Germany to have lunch with Werner Sauer to discuss German chair design of the 1970s and 1980s – a real golden age.

Although many of the chairs in this book were designed by some of the greatest personalities in the design field, a great number of them were and are manufactured anonymously. In these pages the anonymously designed, seemingly uneventful and brutally ugly appear side by side with the elegant and the celebrated.

Certain periods appear to be almost or completely devoid of novel office chairs, such as the 1910s, 20s and 40s. I can only speculate as to whether this is due to our lack of skill as researchers, poorly kept records, a shortage of inspiration among the designers of the time or catastrophes such as the Great Depression, World War I and World War II. Another limitation of this study is that it is restricted to significant and visible novelties in office chair design. There is certainly a history of nuts, bolts, textiles, control buttons and spring coils to be told, but I have chosen not to tell it. Such a history could only be told after a decade of dissecting dozens of office chairs and at the expense of the sanity of those involved.

At the onset of our research Google Patents was still in its infancy, but toward the end of the process it became an instrumental aid in understanding the complex functions of movement mechanisms. We even discovered two chairs from the 1800s that only exist in their patent applications and decided to include them.

Accuracy in this field of research is hampered not only by the several bulwarks already discussed, but also by the very speed and quantity with which mass-manufactured objects are produced. That being said, we cross-referenced multiple opinions and sources before indicating that a design was the first example of this or that feature, released in a specific year, or made of a certain material. In cases where information was lacking, we stated the information we had as accurately as possible. In the catalogue of chairs, if the date of a chair was unknown, we did our best to place it in the correct decade. In the taxonomy, if we knew that something was made of injection-moulded polypropylene the material was stated, but if the type of plastic was uncertain, it was simply left as injection-moulded plastic. The illustrations were made using the best images we could find, so in some cases the views are not ideal or the details were left for us to render as accurately as possible. Any corrections would be gratefully accepted for a future edition if sent to Jonathan Olivares Design Research or to Phaidon Press.

I hope that A Taxonomy of Office Chairs serves as a model for scientific and objective analysis of design history.

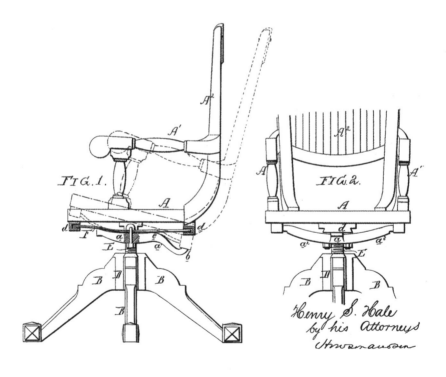

Patent diagram of a 'tilting chair'
Henry S. Hale, United States, 1875

The Evolving Office Chair

In the mid-nineteenth century business management was not yet taught in universities, the first prototypes of calculating machines weighed 15 tons, offices were lit with gaslights, and Windsor chairs were considered acceptable office seating. These circumstances have changed dramatically and office chairs have undergone an extensive design evolution as they have been adapted to the changing world around them.

An interrelated and dynamic set of factors motivates office chair design. Work habits, production technologies, ergonomic ideals, and broad social goals change frequently and considerably and affect the features and functions of office chairs. While an increased concern for consumer safety in the 1970s resulted in the sophisticated chair movement mechanisms of the 1980s and 1990s, our recent preoccupation with sustainability is delivering an array of easily recyclable chairs.

Office chairs have become ubiquitous products, sold in the millions to corporations and institutions the world over. While capitalist society runs on productivity, the human body requires rest and comfort to function optimally, which has guaranteed not only continued business for the office chair industry but also the continued evolution of office chairs.

The advent of the office chair

There is no single inventor of the office chair: the elements that define it – a movement mechanism, adjustable features, and casters – all appeared on different chairs at different times. According to Sigfried Giedion, the roots of the kinetic office chair can be found in the comforts of rural American life. He writes in *Mechanization Takes Command*:

> The American farmer, at the end of the day, will instinctively move to the rocker on his porch. The European peasant sits immovable through the twilight as if nailed to the bench before his cottage. These simple differences must be understood, for more profoundly than one might think, they change the course of inventive fantasy. They underlie the divergence of American and European comfort in the nineteenth century. As soon as mechanization became a decisive power in furniture, these differences began to show.

The first movement mechanisms for office chairs were developed in the United States in the 1840s and 50s with steel coils, cast-iron components and steel leaf springs. Thomas E. Warren's Centripetal Spring Arm-

US Government Bonus Bureau, Computing Division
Washington D.C., 1924

chair of 1849 features arched steel leaf springs that allow the chair to flex in any direction and Peter Ten Eyck's 1853 Sitting Chair has a cast iron pivot point under the seat, which is kept in tension with leaf springs. The earliest known example of a chair on wheels was a William-IV-style armchair modified by Charles Darwin for his study in Kent, England in the 1840s. He replaced the legs of his armchair with cast-iron bed legs mounted on casters so that he could move from specimen to specimen with greater ease. The exact origin of adjustable features is unknown, but by the 1880s CWS Keighley produced models on which the resistance against the reclining of the chair could be adjusted.

These early models anticipated the needs of a changing society. American offices of the early nineteenth century were small and privately owned, until westward railroad expansion allowed businesses to operate in multiple cities and grow into corporations that employed dozens or even hundreds of people. The majority of chairs used in nineteenth-century offices were four-legged dining chairs, but clerical work and factory labor often required extended periods of sitting, for which these chairs were poorly suited. A growing need for mass-produced workplace seating gave manufacturers the social and financial incentive to develop adequate solutions.

Hierarchy in seating

In 1911, Frederick Winslow Taylor, a mechanical engineer and management consultant, published *The Principles of Scientific Management*, which became the foundation of organization for the twentieth-century workplace. Under Taylorist work methods, specific tasks were divided among specialists, who could operate without any awareness of how their work fit into the larger productive efforts of their employer. These workers were often separated spatially and sat in different types of chairs, according to their rank. Hierarchical organization had a long-lasting effect on chair design: from the early-twentieth century up until the 1990s, executives, managers, and secretaries typically sat in chairs that reflected their status.

As well as being more robustly constructed, executive chairs tended to be made using costlier materials and sometimes more sophisticated movement mechanisms than chairs designed for managers or administrative staff. Because each variation had to look and in some cases function differently, hierarchy had an accelerating effect on the evolution of office

Heinz offices
London, 1962

chairs. Frank Lloyd Wright designed separate chairs for the managers and executives of the 1956 Price Tower, the headquarters of an oil pipeline and chemical company in Bartlesville, Oklahoma. A larger base and an adjustable reclining mechanism distinguish the executive chair. The 1979–80 Diffrient series for Knoll is a clear expression of Taylorist hierarchy, with the Executive, Advanced Management, and Basic Operational chairs ranging from largest and most expensive to smallest and least expensive. By the late 1980s, it was common for an office chair series to offer at least three hierarchical distinctions, and sometimes four or five.

In his 1969 book *Utopia or Oblivion*, Buckminster Fuller predicted that the computer would curb the repetitive and specific tasks we associate with scientific management theories such as Taylor's. Since the personal computer became common in offices in the early 1980s, the Taylorist workplace has been slowly dissolving into collaborative and communal organizations of multifaceted workers. It's no coincidence then that the Aeron Chair of 1994, which was developed around postures for computer use, was the first model to deviate from the accepted hierarchical structure. When it was introduced, it was offered in a single color and three sizes designed to accommodate varying body sizes, not indicate varying status levels. If hierarchy is expressed in office chairs today, it is typically done with material; for executive seating, plastics and textiles are often replaced with die-cast aluminium and leather.

Advancements in manufacturing

Production advancements and the development of new materials have changed almost everything about how a chair is made: the heavy cast-iron base was superseded by the lightweight die-cast aluminium base, which was used less frequently after the introduction of the super-light injection-moulded plastic base.

The earliest office chairs were made with wood, cast iron, and steel bar or sheet, and they were upholstered with batting and fabric. In the early twentieth-century materials such as steel tube, sand-cast aluminium, aluminium sheet, and Bakelite began to be employed in chair production. Technologies developed during World War II were applied to office chairs in the decade that followed the war; die-cast aluminium, moulded fibreglass and plastic resin, rubber mounts, industrial-strength glues, and compound-moulded plywood allowed for great

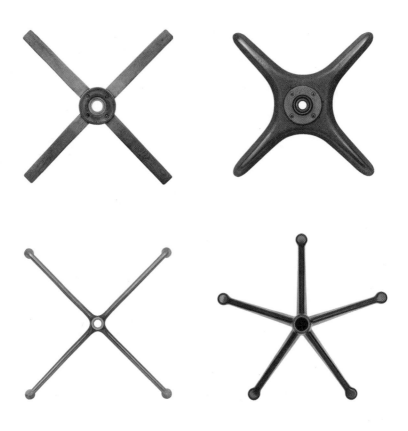

Material evolution of chair bases, 1885–1984
Wood, aluminium, plastic

progress in chair design. In the 1960s, transparent thermoplastic and injection-moulded plastic were first employed on chairs such as the D-49 and Pollock chair. Since then, plastics have undergone a rapid evolution, with frequent introductions of higher-performance plastics. Many variations of injection-moulded plastic with a plethora of physical properties have been released since the 1970s, and there isn't an office chair on the market today that doesn't employ some form of this material.

As production processes have become more advanced and chairs more complex, the initial investment required to produce the tools to manufacture a chair has greatly increased. Such tools are only accessible to furniture companies with millions of dollars of annual revenue and suitable distribution networks. Most of the family-owned office furniture businesses are gone as a result, and there are fewer opportunities for makers of bespoke chairs.

Sigmund Freud's office chair was custom-made, as were the chairs that Frank Lloyd Wright designed for his various buildings. Over time custom jobs became less frequent, or they were only used to develop a chair in a test environment that could eventually be distributed to a larger market. The padded leather chair Charles and Ray Eames designed for the lobby and executive floors of the Time-Life building in New York City in 1960 has also been sold to the public by its manufacturer Herman Miller ever since.

The ergonomic office

By the 1970s, designers such as Niels Diffrient, Wolfgang Müeller Deisig and Bill Stumpf were designing chairs that supported the contours of the body with moulded polyurethane foam. Much of the focus of office chair design had shifted to ergonomics, as information gathered about the human body during the war entered the public domain and was widely published in books such as Henry Dreyfuss's *Measure of Man* (1960) and Diffrient's *Humanscale* (1974).

At this time an increased public demand for consumer health led to raised safety standards in everything from packaged food and automobiles to office chairs. By the late 1980s the Council of the European Union had begun to put legislation in place that demanded minimum ergonomic standards be met in the workplace, and forced manufacturers to make suitable designs. Despite the lack of similar legislation enforcing ergonomic

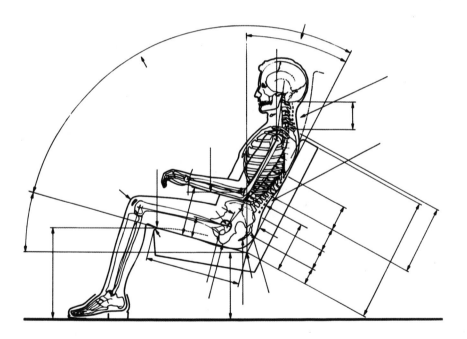

'Seated 50th percentile male' from the book *Humanscale*
Niels Diffrient, MIT Press, 1974

design in the American workplace, US corporations soon realized that it was less expensive to buy ergonomic office chairs than to pay higher insurance rates to cover workers suffering from back and neck injuries.

When the personal computer was introduced to offices in the 1980s professionals began spending significantly longer periods of time seated at their desks. Before personal computers, files and machines were located throughout the office, and employees would move around far more than they do with their own PC. While the ergonomic design of the 1970s and early 80s focused on supporting the body, ergonomic design from the mid 80s on focused on supporting the body for eight consecutive hours of seated PC use. Extended seated time only heightened the regulations placed on chair ergonomics by governments and insurance companies, and as a result the 1990s and 2000s saw an explosion of ergonomically designed chairs.

A checklist of features that determines whether or not a chair is ergonomic and safe enough first emerged in the late 1980s and has continued to expand. These features vary from institution to institution and country to country, but some common elements are height- and depth-adjustable armrests, depth-adjustable seats, height-adjustable lumbar supports, and large quintuple bases for stability. The adjustable features are required to accommodate varying body sizes, but all these extra features and additional mechanisms tend to make office chairs more robust, and have contributed to the gradual increase in size of the office chair over the last twenty years.

Sustainability and the shifting workplace

Although the search for new ergonomic solutions continues to motivate the design of office chairs, the factor that has contributed most to recent changes in how they are made is sustainability. European and American office chair manufacturers are striving to eliminate aspects of the manufacturing process that are harmful to the environment, such as volatile organic compound emissions, hazardous waste, and waste to landfills. This affects not only the materials used, but also how the chairs are assembled. One of the first office chairs to be promoted as a sustainable design was the Mirra of 2003. It is 96 percent recyclable by weight, made with 42 percent recycled content, and is designed to disassemble easily for recycling or to have its parts replaced.

Various postures supported by the Generation chair
Designed by Formway for Knoll, 2009

This move toward sustainability has been accompanied by a tendency to make office chairs support a range of postures, from leaning or sitting sideways to sitting backward. Today's mobile devices allow us to work just about anywhere and in any position. In 2009 three chairs were released that accommodate a broader range of movement: the ON allows users to shift their weight from side to side, the Generation encourages them to sit sideways or backwards, and the 360° has no fixed orientation, enabling the user to adopt any number of postures. These chairs encourage human interaction and accommodate the collaborative spirit of contemporary offices.

Societal change and the future of office seating

The office chair has evolved through four key phases. During its first phase in the nineteenth century, designers invented the office chair archetype and the movement mechanism to suit the needs of expanding businesses. The early twentieth century and immediate post-war years ushered in a range of new materials and manufacturing technologies that industrialized chair production, taking it away from its craft origins. A third phase, beginning in the 1970s and ending only recently, brought about ergonomically advanced office chairs designed for sitting at computers for extended periods. Finally, we see the introduction of sustainable chairs that suit the shifting and impromptu postures adopted by today's workforce. In the span of seven generations of office workers, the office chair has evolved into a complex organism. Despite this healthy evolution, the office chair's natural habitat – the office – is anything but stable. The contemporary workplace is undergoing transformations of its own as more work is brought into the cloud: we can only speculate what will happen as an increasing number of people work from home, as 40 percent of IBM's employees do now, and mobile devices continue to allow us to work without a fixed location. As specialized a subject as the office chair may be, its evolution and story are indicative of the broad and rapid changes that our society has undergone and will continue to undergo.

Catalogue of Chairs

Sitting Chair

Peter Ten Eyck
USA
1853

The seat tilts backward and pivots from its central connection to the stem. Backward-tilting in office chairs is thought to have evolved from the American rocking chair.

Backrest pp92, 123, Armrest p128, Seat p157, Seat-Stem Joinery p174, Movement p201

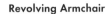

Revolving Armchair

Gebrüder Thonet, Austria
1865

The backrest and seat are constructed of rattan weave in a bentwood frame. In 1994 this construction technique inspired the semi-transparent backrest and seat of the now ubiquitous Aeron Chair.

Backrest p104, Armrest p138, Seat p164, Stem p179, Base p185, Floor Contact p196

Improved Office Chair

Robert Fitts
USA
1867

The seat, backrest and armrests tilt backward on bilateral pivot points at the rear of the seat. A tension spring under the seat resists the sitter's weight and a threaded stem allows the height of the chair to be adjusted.

Seat-Stem Joinery p174, Movement p202

Centripetal Spring Armchair

Thomas E. Warren
American Chair Company, USA
1849

The headrest, armrests and base are made of cast iron, a material that would become standard in office chair production during the following decades. Eight flexing bands of bowed steel join the stem to the base, and allow the chair to flex in any direction under the sitter's weight.

Headrest pp83, 86, Backrest p95, Armrest pp130, 138, Seat p159, Seat-Stem Joinery p168, Stem p181, Base p185, Floor Contact p193, Movement p200

Unknown 1

Singer Manufacturing Company, USA
1872

The base is cast in iron as a monobloc with four articulated legs. Monobloc bases have become standard in office chairs and today are made of injection-moulded plastics or die-cast aluminium.

Backrest p118, Seat-Stem Joinery p168, Stem p179, Base p185, Movement p203

Revolving Rocking Armchair

Gebrüder Thonet, Austria
1885

The armrests are closed loops of bentwood. Many subsequent office chairs have closed-loop armrests and the feature has been executed in many other materials.

Armrest p149

Unknown 2

CWS Keighley, England
1885

Three turning knobs control backrest height, backrest angle and seat tilt tension. Adjustable features accommodate varying body sizes in a wide range of users.

Backrest p112, Seat-Stem Joinery p171, Base p185

Office Chair No. 982

Sears Roebuck, USA
1897

The slatted wooden backrest and a compact tilt mechanism are simplifications of features found on precedent office chairs. Reduction of labour and materials were necessary for the Sears Roebuck catalogue to sell the chair at low cost.

Backrest p123, Armrest p138, Seat-Stem Joinery p168

Larkin Building Chair

Frank Lloyd Wright
Von Dorn Iron Works Company, USA
1904

The perforated backrest and the armrests are constructed with folded sheet steel, and five cast-iron stems join the base and seat. Like Wright's other chairs made for specific buildings, this design was never mass-produced.

Backrest pp92, 116, Armrest pp128, 138, Stem p181

Unknown 3

Singer Manufacturing Company, USA
1925

The base is a cast-iron pyramidal monobloc and the wooden seat and backrest are joined by a bent steel bar. Singer manufactured chairs to be used with their sewing machines and tables.

Backrest p112, Base p183

Sigmund Freud's Office Chair

Karl Hofmann and Felix Augenfeld
Austria
1926

A narrow upholstered backrest with a pronounced headrest
is supported by the armrests. Sigmund Freud commissioned
Hofmann and Augenfeld to create this chair for his office.

Headrest p86, Backrest pp95, 116, Armrest pp130, 139

Federdreh

Albert Stoll II
Giroflex, Switzerland
1928

The stem is a steel tube that passes through a wooden base
and rotates 360 degrees within it. A spring coil around the stem
gives the seat a slight bounce. By the 1970s bounce is provided
by pneumatic cylinders.

Seat-Stem Joinery p174, Stem p179

Drehstuhl

Walter Funkat
Hinz Fabrik, Germany
1929

The backrest pivots on steel fittings that join it to the bilateral
wooden supports.

Backrest p118

B7a

Marcel Breuer
Gëbruder Thonet, Austria
1928

The backrest, armrests and base are made with bent steel
tubes. Steel tubes are still employed in office chairs today.
The stretched fabric of the backrest informs many subsequent
chair designs, including the Aluminum Group Chair.

*Backrest p104, Armrest p139, Seat-Stem Joinery p174,
Stem p179, Base p186*

Maharaja

Jacques-Emile Ruhlmann
France
1929

The chair sits on a massive base made of metal and wood veneer and the upholstered backrest is upheld by the armrests. The chair was commissioned by the Maharaja of Indore.

Backrest p124, Armrest p132, Base p183

Polstergleich

Margarete Klöber
Klöber, Germany
1935

The movement mechanism is raised on four compact springs which allow it to flex and sink slightly in any direction.

Seat-Stem Joinery p175

S.C. Johnson & Son Building Armchair

Frank Lloyd Wright
Metal Office Furniture Company / Steelcase, USA
1937

The base is made of a framework of metal tubes and the seat adjusts forward and backward along the base. The armrests are not supported at the sides of the seat which leaves space to allow the sitter to shift his or her legs to the side.

Armrest p142, Seat-Stem Joinery p173, Stem p181, Base p184

Montecatini Headquarters Chair

Gio Ponti
Kardex Italiano, Italy
1938

The base is a single piece of die-cast aluminium, which became a common production method for chair bases. The backrest and seat are Bakelite, the first true plastic. Plastic has since become a standard material in office seating.

Backrest pp92, 118, Seat p157, Base p186

Custom Adjustable Chair

Warren McArthur
Warren McArthur Corporation, USA
1930s

This chair is constructed of aluminium tubes, plate, and castings and upholstered in vinyl. The headrest height, and the depth and angle of the backrest are adjustable.

Headrest p87, Backrest p123, Armrest pp130, 148, Floor Contact p196

Steno Posture Chair

Emeco, USA
1944

Two aluminium spines, bent from the same length, hold the backrest panel, which is made with batting and vinyl glued to an aluminium panel.

Backrest pp95, 118, Seat p159

71 Saarinen Armchair

Eero Saarinen
Knoll, USA
1951

An upholstered, moulded fibreglass shell forms the armrests and backrest. Moulded fibreglass allowed for contoured shapes that traditional materials such as wood and steel did not.

Backrest pp95, 124, Armrest p132, Seat p159

Flying Duck Chair

George Nelson
Herman Miller, USA
1955

The armrests are connected to the sides of the seat along its entire length and angle outward at their highest point.

Armrest p132

Model 3107

Arne Jacobsen
Fritz Hansen, Denmark
1955

Each plywood armrest is supported by a cantilevered steel rod that is fixed to the underside of the seat. This structural configuration is employed in many subsequent office chairs.

Backrest p108, Armrest p147, Base p188, Floor Contact p193

PACC

Charles and Ray Eames
Herman Miller, USA / Vitra, Switzerland
1953

A moulded shell of fibreglass and plastic resin available in bright colors forms the backrest, armrests and seat. Optional contoured upholstery covers the front face of the shell and a plastic extrusion seals the edges. Narrow die-cast aluminium legs have a hollow, ribbed underside for added structure.

Backrest pp92, 96, 108, 111, Armrest pp128, 130, 135, Seat pp157, 159, Stem p180, Base p186, Floor Contact p196

PP 502

Hans J. Wegner
Johannes Hansen Møbelsnedkeri / PP Møbler, Denmark
1955

The curvaceous backrest-armrest structure is milled from solid
wood and supported by three steel tube spines. The base
is made of a truss of steel tubes.

Backrest p116, Armrest p139, Base p188

Price Tower Armchair

Frank Lloyd Wright
Blue Stem Foundry, USA
1956

A sand cast aluminium spine joins the backrest to the base.
The angular geometries of the chairs designed by Wright for
the Price Tower in Oklahoma resemble the interior spaces.

Backrest p116, Armrest p139, Base p183

Price Tower Executive Armchair

Frank Lloyd Wright
Blue Stem Foundry, USA
1956

The base is a dodecagon of sand-cast aluminium with reliefs,
and the armrests are closed loops of the same material.

Backrest pp96, 115, Base p183

Aluminum Group Chair

Charles and Ray Eames
Herman Miller, USA / Vitra, Switzerland
1958

The backrest and seat are constructed with fabric stretched between die-cast aluminium spines, which are spread apart by a die-cast aluminium handle on the backrest and four steel bars in the seat-stem joinery. Loop-shaped armrests are fixed to the bilateral frames at three raised points.

Backrest pp104, 119, Armrest pp128, 149, Seat p164, Seat-Stem Joinery p175, Base p189, Floor Contact p193

DAF Chair

George Nelson
Herman Miller, USA / Vitra, Switzerland
1958

A moulded fibreglass backrest-armrest structure is attached to an armrest-seat shell of the same material.

Backrest p124, Armrest p132, Stem p180, Base p186

Kevi

Jørgen Rasmussen
Kevi, Denmark
1958

The plastic double casters move more fluidly than single casters. Known as Kevi casters, they became an industry standard. An updated model of this design produced in 1978 featured height adjustable armrests, which are now a feature of most office chairs.

Armrest p143, Floor Contact p194

MAA Chair

George Nelson
Herman Miller, USA / Vitra, Switzerland
1958

The backrest is attached to the armrest-seat shell with die-cast aluminium lengths and flexing rubber mounts, which allow it to tilt backward.

Backrest p124, Armrest p133, Movement p204

Unknown 4

France
1950s

Cast-aluminium armrests in a double post formation support
upholstered pads.

Backrest p115, Armrest p148

Time-Life Chair

Charles and Ray Eames
Herman Miller, USA / Vitra, Switzerland
1960

The upholstered armrests are raised from their die-cast aluminium supports. This chair was designed for the lobby and
executive floors of the Time-Life building in New York City.

Armrest p149

D-49

Hans Könecke
Tecta, Germany
1964

The backrest, armrests and seat are made of heat-pressed
transparent thermoplastic (PMMA) and fastened together
with hardware.

Backrest p96, Armrest pp129, 133, Seat p160

FK 6725 Bucket Chair

Preben Fabricius and Jørgen Kastholm
Alfred Kill International, Germany
1965

The base is a three-legged cast-aluminium monobloc. Three-legged bases are unstable, and have been banned from European and North American offices by safety standards commissions since the 1970s.

Base p184

Pollock Chair

Charles Pollock
Knoll, USA
1965

The backrest-seat shell is made of injection-moulded plastic and its edge is finished with an extruded aluminium profile. This chair was designed to use fifty percent less fabric than Knoll's 71 Series from 1951, and therefore cost less.

Backrest pp96, 108, Armrest pp129, 149, Seat p160

Pearson Executive Chair

Max Pearson
Knoll, USA
1966

Chrome steel caps placed on top of the base prevent it from scuffing. The base was used on several of Knoll's subsequent chairs, and a five-legged version is still in production today.

Base p187

Model 1904

Jørgen Rasmussen
Knoll, USA
1967

A die-cast aluminium bracket with four splayed lengths
connect the seat and stem.

Seat-Stem Joinery p175

232

Wilhelm Ritz
Wilkhahn, Germany
1970

A pneumatic cylinder in the stem adjusts the seat height when
activated by a lever. Borrowed from automotive trunks, this
component replaced the threaded fitting that required a user
to rotate the entire chair to adjust the height.

Backrest p119, Stem p180, Floor Contact p194

Light

George Nelson
Herman Miller, USA
1970

The inner backrest and seat are made with elastic rubber
sheets, suspended from a steel frame with springs. This
advanced suspension forms a technological link between the
Revolving Armchair of 1865 and the Aeron Chair of 1994.

Backrest p105, Seat p164

Archizoom Uno

Archizoom (Paolo Deganello and Gilberto Coretti)
Marcatré, Italy
1973

Fabric is stretched around a steel tube armrest-backrest structure and attached to the underside of the seat. This design advances the tube-fabric combination of the B7a of 1928 by adding contour to support the lower back.

Backrest p105, Seat-Stem Joinery p171

Morrison / Hannah Task Chair

Andrew Ivar Morrison and Bruce R. Hannah
Knoll, USA
1973

Die-cast aluminium armrests wrap behind and support a flexible die-cut plastic sheet, overmoulded with a PU foam cushion. The flexing backrest and seatfront achieve a highly responsive level of movement with rudimentary means.

Backrest pp97, 125, Seat p160

Vertebra

Emilio Ambasz and Giancarlo Piretti
Castelli, Italy
1974

A segmented backrest is supported by a bilateral structure of flexing steel tube and spring-loaded hinges, which are covered in rubber bellows. The cushions are made with polyurethane foam with a moisture-resistant outer skin.

Backrest pp97, 125, Armrest pp129, 140, Seat p160

Synthesis 45

Ettore Sottsass Jr
Olivetti, Italy
1973

The base is made of injection-moulded ABS plastic and the
single spine that holds the backrest is made with the same
material. Most office chairs now have plastic bases.

Backrest p112, Stem p180, Base p187

238/7

Delta Design
Wilkhahn, Germany
1976

The backrest consists of three vertically segmented cushions intended to provide support to different areas of the back.

Backrest pp97, 112

Beaubourg

Michel Cadestin and George Laurent
Teda, France
1976

The seat and backrest are each a framework of welded steel rods. This chair was designed for the offices of the Centre Pompidou and was subsequently sold to the public.

Backrest p97, Seat p161, Base p188

Ergon

William Stumpf
Herman Miller, USA
1976

The contoured backrest and seat are made of cold-moulded polyurethane foam and covered with a stretch fabric that is heat-pressed and glued to the foam.

Backrest pp98, 115, Seat p161, Floor Contact pp194, 197

MKD

Jørgen Rasmussen
Herman Miller, USA
1976

An injection-moulded backrest-armrest structure is a technical advancement on the backrest-armrest structure of the PP 502 of 1955.

Backrest p117, Armrest p140

Mister

Bruno Mathsson
Bruno Mathsson International, Sweden
1977

The seat and stem are connected with bilateral steel tubes that cantilever forward from the stem and bend backward into the seat front. The seat flexes downward from its foremost region.

Headrest p89, Seat-Stem Joinery p171, Base p187

Rollback Chair

Ray Wilkes
Herman Miller, USA
1977

The backrest is an upholstered moulded foam cylinder that rotates on a single steel tube, allowing the user to adjust backrest depth.

Backrest pp98, 113, Armrest p143, Base p187

Fysio

Yrjö Kukkapurro
Avarte, Finland
1978

A moulded-plywood headrest panel adjusts vertically along
the backrest panel.

Headrest pp83, 86

Sapper Chair

Richard Sapper
Knoll, USA
1978

Rolled steel 'U' sections create an internal structure between
the backrest and seat. This production technique was taken
from the automotive bumper industry. Batting and leather cover
the structure and are closed with a plastic band.

Backrest p119, Armrest p136

Diffrient Advanced Management

Niels Diffrient
Knoll, USA
1979

The seat-backrest shell is a single piece of stamped steel with
an upholstered polyurethane cushion. The moulded contours
of the foam are based on the ergonomics explored in Diffrient's
Humanscale books.

*Backrest pp98, 108, Seat p161, Seat-Stem Joinery p168,
Base p189*

Vitramat

Wolfgang Müeller Deisig
Vitra, Switzerland
1976

The backrest and its single supporting spine are integrated into a continuous upholstered surface. The polyurethane foam cushions of the backrest and seat are moulded directly on to the fabric.

Backrest pp98, 113, Seat p161

Diffrient Executive Highback

Niels Diffrient
Knoll, USA
1979

In recline, the upper backrest cushion is tilted forward by the armrests to support the sitter's upper back.

Armrest p140

Supporto

Fred Scott
Hille, England
1979

The backrest tilts backward on a broad spring-loaded joint that connects it to the seat.

Backrest p109

454 ConCentrx

Steelcase Design Studio
Steelcase, USA
1980

The backrest and seat are made with two-part flexing plastic panels that allow the upper portion of the backrest to flex backward and the front of the seat to flex downward.

Backrest p99, Armrest p143, Seat p162

Diffrient Basic Operational Chair

Niels Diffrient
Knoll, USA
1980

The backrest is depth and height adjustable along its single supporting spine. A gas cylinder activated with a button on the armrest adjusts the chair's height.

Backrest p113, Armrest p143

Milton High

Bruno Mathsson
Bruno Mathsson International, Sweden
1980

The headrest cushion is a separate upholstered element attached to the backrest-headrest panel with a strap. Several subsequent headrests are designed as separate elements.

Headrest p85, Backrest p111, Armrest p135

Stephens High Back Executive

William Stephens
Knoll, USA
1980

The backrest and armrests are attached beneath the seat with single depth-adjustable lengths of bent steel.

Backrest p113, Armrest p144

Dorsal

Emilio Ambasz and Giancarlo Piretti
KI, USA
1982

The armrests are attached to the underside of the seat front and cantilever backward. The upper backrest is connected to the lower backrest on spring-loaded joints covered in rubber bellows.

Backrest p120, Armrest p144

Kevi 2

Jørgen Rasmussen
Kevi, Denmark
1982

The backrest is held by the vertical posts that support the armrests.

Backrest p119, Floor Contact p196

Capisco

Peter Opsvik
HÅG, Norway
1984

The headrest is depth and height adjustable, the narrow backrest forms short armrests, and the casters are covered with footrests. The design allows a user to sit sideways and facing backward.

Headrest p87, Armrest p136, Base p191

FS Chair

Klaus Franck, Werner Sauer and Fritz Frenkler
Wilkhahn, Germany
1980

Four pivoting points, including a flexing area at the vertex of
the plastic armrest, facilitate seat and backrest recline. This
mechanism is the first to provide simultaneous, yet distinct
movement on the backrest and seat. The seat is constructed with
rubber netting stretched from front to back over a steel frame.

*Armrest p140, Seat p165, Seat-Stem Joinery p173,
Movement p205*

Credo

Peter Opsvik
HÅG, Norway
1984

The height-adjustable armrests are supported by posts at the front of the chair. The ends of the base are covered with plastic caps to suggest footrests.

Armrest p144, Base p191

Figura

Mario Bellini
Vitra, Switzerland
1984

The upholstery on the backrest is held in place by a band of fabric wrapped around the lower backrest.

Backrest p99

Helena Chair

Niels Diffrient
Sunar-Hauserman, USA
1984

The backrest of this chair is held by the armrests on pivoting joints.

Backrest p125, Armrest p144

Persona

Mario Bellini
Vitra, Switzerland
1984

A die-cast aluminium tilt mechanism is located between the cushion and the flexible plastic panel of the backrest-seat. The intention was to reduce the size of the mechanism and remove it from the user's sight.

Backrest p99, Seat p162, Base p189

System 25

Richard Sapper
Comforto, Germany
1984

As in the FS Chair of 1980, four pivoting points facilitate seat and backrest recline, however in this design the point at the front of the armrest pivots mechanically instead of flexing.

Armrest p141

Sensor

Wolfgang Müeller Deisig
Steelcase, USA
1986

An internal flexing steel spine runs along the center of the backrest-seat and allows the backrest to flex backward.

Backrest p109

Kite

Foster + Partners
Tecno, Italy
1987

The backrest, seat, and seat-stem joinery are all made of folded sheet steel. This manufacturing approach was inspired by car body construction.

Backrest p100, Seat p162, Seat-Stem Joinery p175

AC 1

Antonio Citterio
Vitra, Switzerland
1988

The backrest extends below the seat, where it attaches to and engages the movement mechanism. The recline follows a similar movement as the FS Chair of 1980.

Backrest p117, Armrest p141, Seat-Stem Joinery p172

Criterion

Steelcase Design Studio
Steelcase, USA
1989

The span between the armrests is adjustable and makes this chair suitable for large users.

Armrest p145

Equa Chair

William Stumpf and Donald Chadwick
Herman Miller, USA
1984

The movement mechanism that joins the seat to the stem is positioned under the front of the seat, allowing the sitter's feet to stay on the ground as his or her body tilts backward and sinks downward from the knees. Referred to as 'knee tilt' this movement method is refined in Stumpf and Chadwick's Aeron Chair, in which they achieve 'ankle tilt.'

Backrest pp99, 120, Seat p162, Seat-Stem Joinery p171, Floor Contact p197, Movement p206

Hollington Chair

Geoff Hollington
Herman Miller, USA
1989

The armrests form one continuous element with the lower backrest.

Backrest pp100, 111, Armrest pp131, 135

AC 2

Antonio Citterio
Vitra, Switzerland
1990

The backrest is made of rattan suspended over a die-cast aluminium frame and represents a technological advancement of the rattan backrests of Thonet chairs from the late 1800s.

Backrest p105, Floor Contact p197

Picto

ProduktEntwicklung Roericht
Hans Roericht, Burkard Schmitz, Franz Bigel
Wilkhahn, Germany
1991

As the sitter leans back, a lever redirects the force of the movement to raise and move the seat forward. The weight placed on the seat resists this lever and automatically adjusts the stiffness of the chair's recline to the sitter's weight.

Backrest p93, Seat-Stem Joinery p169, Movement p207

Vertair

Emilio Ambasz
Castelli, Italy
1991

An internal spring-loaded mechanism allows the upper region of the backrest to pivot backward.

Backrest pp100, 109, Armrest p145

Zackback

Dennis Zacharkow
Yogaback, USA
1992

A continuous bilateral frame made of steel tubes holds two height-adjustable cushions that allow for a range of back support. The lower cushion is intended to support the sacral region of the back.

Backrest pp100, 120

Incisa

Vico Magistretti
De Padova, Italy
1994

A continuous backrest-armrest structure is made with leather and upholstery, and was inspired by riding saddle construction.

Backrest p111, Armrest p135, Base p189

Modus

Klaus Franck, Werner Sauer and Wiege
Wilkhahn, Germany
1994

The headrest is made of fabric stretched around an injection-moulded nylon and glass frame.

Headrest pp84, 89, Armrest p142

Soho

Roberto Lucci and Paolo Orlandini
Knoll, USA
1994

The base is shaped for optimal strength and structure, as its material, glass-reinforced nylon, had not been used for a base before. It is now the most commonly used plastic for bases.

Seat-Stem Joinery p169, Base p190

T Chair

Antonio Citterio
Vitra, Switzerland
1994

The backrest of the chair is covered with a three-dimensional knitted textile. Several subsequent backrests employ this technique and the technology is applied to the armrests of the Worknest chair of 2006.

Backrest p101, Armrest p145

Aeron Chair

William Stumpf and Donald Chadwick
Herman Miller, USA
1994

The seat and backrest are made with a semi-transparent
woven plastic and fabric mesh moulded into glass-reinforced
nylon frames. Four pivot points in the movement mechanism
advance the seat recline the designers achieved with the
Equa Chair of 1984. A lumbar support adjusts vertically
behind the backrest.

*Backrest pp105, 120, Armrest p136, Lumbar Support
pp151, 153, Seat p165, Seat-Stem Joinery p176,
Floor Contact p195, Movement p208*

Avian Work Chair

Tom Newhouse
Herman Miller, USA
1995

The backrest is supported by a spine and armrests made with glass-reinforced nylon.

Backrest p117

Axess

Antonio Citterio
Vitra, Switzerland
1996

Upholstery covers the upper half of the backside of the backrest and conceals an adjustable lumbar support panel within the backrest.

Backrest p101, Lumbar Support p155, Seat-Stem Joinery p177

Juli

Werner Aisslinger
Cappellini, Italy
1996

The backrest, armrests and seat are made from a single piece of moulded integral polyurethane foam, which is soft and is slightly flexible.

Backrest pp93, 109, Armrest pp129, 133, Seat p157, Seat-Stem Joinery p169

Meda Chair

Alberto Meda
Vitra, Switzerland
1996

The seat is fixed to an aluminium frame at its sides and rear while its front remains flexible. The backrest reclines from two pivoting points and is upheld by a spring that adjusts for varying resistance against the sitter's recline.

Seat p165, Seat-Stem Joinery p173

Spin

Ross Lovegrove
Driade, Italy
1997

This seat-armrest-backrest structure offers a technological update on the DAF Chair of 1958; the seat-armrest is made of polypropylene and the armrest-backrest is made of a translucent opaline.

Backrest pp93, 125, Armrest p133

Meda2

Alberto Meda
Vitra, Switzerland
1998

An injection-moulded polyamide headrest (not pictured) with a techno-gel cushion clips on to the backrest. The lumbar support is suspended between two layers of mesh stretched across the backrest frame.

Headrest pp83, 87, Armrest p145, Lumbar Support p155

Tris

Emilio Ambasz
Emilio Ambasz & Associates, Inc., USA
1998

A segmented backrest is supported by and pivots on bilateral steel spines.

Backrest p121, Lumbar Support p153

Ypsilon

Mario and Claudio Bellini
Vitra, Switzerland
1998

The headrest is a hollow backless cushion made of a moulded Thermolast K TPE plastic. The backrest is a flexible translucent thermoplastic pad held at four points by extensions of the backrest spine.

Headrest pp83, 88, Backrest p106, Lumbar Support p152

Caper Chair

William Stumpf and Jeff Weber
Herman Miller, USA
1999

The plastic backrest fits on to two bilateral steel tubes, and the chair's armrests flex downward in their foremost area.

Backrest pp93, 126, Seat p158, Seat-Stem Joinery p173, Base 190

Freedom

Niels Diffrient
Humanscale, USA
1999

The headrest tilts forward as the sitter reclines, keeping the head in an upright position. The armrests adjust simultaneously, as they pivot off the double spine which supports the backrest.

Headrest p89, Armrest pp131, 142, Seat p163, Seat-Stem Joinery p176

Leap

IDEO and Steelcase Design Studio
Steelcase, USA
1999

The depth of the lower-back support is adjusted by turning a knob which controls the tension of a slotted, flexing polypropylene backrest panel.

Backrest pp101, 126, Armrest p146

H05

Peter Opsvik
HÅG, Norway
2000

The armrests swing around behind the backrest from a pivoting joint below the seat.

Armrest p146

Open Up

Mathias Seiler
Sedus, Germany
2001

The headrest pivots backward on spring-loaded bilateral hinges.

Headrest p89

Cachet

Peter Jon Pearce
Steelcase, USA
2002

The backrest is a flexing, slotted plastic panel and the seat is a flexing perforated panel with an integral rigid frame.

Backrest p94, Seat p158

Contessa

Giorgetto Giugiaro
Okamura, Japan
2002

The seat is depth adjustable on four rolling gears. Bilateral knobs control the depth of the lumbar support.

Headrest p88, Armrest p147, Lumbar Support p154

.04

Maarten van Severen
Vitra, Switzerland
2000

The backrest-seat panel is made of moulded polyurethane
foam over a steel frame. The seat-stem joinery is mounted to
the stem around a flexible rubber fitting that allows the chair
to tilt slightly with the user's weight.

*Backrest pp106, 121, Armrest p148, Seat p165,
Seat-Stem Joinery p172*

Leap Worklounge

IDEO and Steelcase Design Studio
Steelcase, USA
2002

The headrest and lower back support are made with loosely attached pillows, a technique borrowed from lounge chairs.

Headrest p85, Lumbar Support p152

Liberty

Niels Diffrient
Humanscale, USA
2002

Three pieces of mesh fabric are sewn together along contoured seams that sculpt the fabric in the frame to support the lower back.

Backrest p106, Armrest p136, Floor Contact p195

Life

Formway
Knoll, USA
2002

The seat cushion sits on top of a perforated plastic sheet which flexes under the sitter's weight.

Seat p163, Floor Contact p195

Perpetual 4300 Series

William Goodworth
Hon, USA
2002

The backrest is supported by bilateral spines which coil into a flexing spring under the seat and provide backrest tilt when the user reclines.

Backrest p121

Solis

Weige
Wilkhahn, Germany
2002

This chair's headrest consists of an upholstered pad that rests on a plastic panel.

Headrest pp86, 90

Duo Back

Martin Ballendat
Rohde & Grahl, Germany
2003

The separate panels of the backrest flex independently of each other.

Backrest pp101, 121

Giroflex 63

Zemp + Partner Design
Giroflex, Switzerland
2003

The single spine that supports the backrest tilts forward,
collapsing the backrest on to the seat for compact storage
or shipping.

Backrest p114

Mirra Chair

Studio 7.5
Herman Miller, USA
2003

The backrest is a flexible, contoured, perforated panel of plastic
held at four points by extensions of the backrest spine. The
depth of the seat can be adjusted by raising or lowering the
foremost area of the seat with a handle below it.

Backrest pp94, 102, 115, Lumbar Support pp151, 154,
Seat p166

Orbit

Eckard Hansen and Gerhard Reichert
Klöber, Germany
2003

The elliptical headrest cushion is held with bilateral arms that
allow it to rotate 360 degrees.

Headrest p90, Armrest p137

Spoon Chair

Antonio Citterio
Kartell, Italy
2003

The seat is cantilevered backward on a flexible plastic panel which joins it to the stem and provides a basic seat recline.

Backrest p110, Armrest p137, Seat-Stem Joinery p169

Xten

Pininfarina
Ares Line, Italy
2003

The headrest is constructed of mesh in a moulded plastic frame. This frame is supported by two steel cylinders which raise and lower into the plastic volume that spans the height of the backrest.

Headrest pp84, 90, Armrest p137

H09

Svein Asbjørnsen and sapDesign
HÅG, Norway
2004

The backrest's mesh is stretched between two horizontal posts at the top and bottom of the backrest. A lumbar support and headrest are positioned behind the mesh and supported by a central spine.

Headrest p87, Backrest p106, Armrest p146

Tacit

Isao Hosoe
Itoki, Japan
2004

The backrest is attached to a single spine with a pivoting joint which allows it to be tilted on its side and used as an armrest.

Backrest p114

Celle

Jerome Caruso
Herman Miller, USA
2005

The backrest and seat of this chair are injection-moulded plastic panels with three-dimensional patterns of flexing points.

Backrest p94, Seat p158

Chadwick

Donald Chadwick
Knoll, USA
2005

The armrest's post splits and connects to the back and front of the armrest platform. The height of the armrest can be adjusted with the use of an interior ratchet.

Armrest p147, Lumbar Support p155

Think

Glen Oliver Low with Steelcase Design Studio
Steelcase, USA
2004

The chair is ninety-eight percent recyclable by weight and designed to be disassembled using basic hand tools in five minutes. The movement mechanism is built using four steel-leaf springs giving the chair a similar movement pattern to the Picto of 1991. Steel springs had not been used for a movement mechanism since the 1840s and 1850s.

Backrest p107, Seat p166, Seat-Stem Joinery p176

Headline

Mario and Claudio Bellini
Vitra, Switzerland
2005

A double spine made of die-cast aluminium is attached to the lower backrest and headrest at hinged joints. As the user reclines the hinged joints tilt the headrest forward, ensuring that the user's line of sight remains constant.

Headrest p90, Backrest p122

Lotus

Jasper Morrison
Cappellini, Italy
2006

The headrest is a removable cushion attached to the backrest magnetically.

Headrest p85

Otto Chair

Antonio Citterio and Toan Nguyen
B&B Italia, Italy
2006

The backrest is made with thermoplastic overmoulded with a flexible translucent plastic.

Backrest p94

Permiso

IDEO with Vecta
Vecta, USA
2006

The armrests fold outward, allowing the user to sit sideways with their legs over the side of the seat.

Armrest p134

Rolling Frame

Alberto Meda
Alias, Italy
2006

A thin arc of die-cast aluminium provides two connections between the stem and the rear of the seat, while two robust die-cast aluminium arms cantilever forward from the stem and flow into the seat frame.

Seat-Stem Joinery p176

Sguig

EOOS
Keilhauer, Canada
2006

A die-cast aluminium spine supports a flexible Hytrel backrest which allows the user's shoulders to push backward.

Backrest pp102, 114

Worknest

Ronan and Erwan Bouroullec
Vitra, Switzerland
2006

The height adjustment mechanism of the armrest is concealed by a three-dimensonally knitted cover that continues into the seat. This cover has elastic properties that allow it to stay taut and maintain a consistent silhouette as the armrest is raised and lowered.

Armrest p134

Cpod

Allseating, Canada
2007

Horizontal straps which span the width of the backrest frame control the contour and depth of the backrest, and are adjusted with ratchets along the frame.

Backrest p107, Lumbar Support p154

Diffrient World

Niels Diffrient
Humanscale
2008

The backrest of this chair lifts and tilts the seat as the sitter reclines, as with other chairs, but does so with minimal components that include a double spine in the backrest connected to a single bracket under the seat.

Backrest p122, Seat-Stem Joinery p172

360°

Konstantin Grcic
Magis, Italy
2009

This typology was designed without a single orientation, allowing the user to sit in a variety of postures.

Backrest p102, Armrest p131, Seat p163, Seat-Stem Joinery p170, Base p191

Cobi

Luke Pearson, PearsonLloyd with Steelcase Design Studio
Steelcase, USA
2009

The plastic backrest is perforated with vertical slots, which make it flexible, and its height is finished with a soft plastic band that flexes under a sitter's arm. The front face of the backrest is covered with a semi-transparent fabric.

Backrest p102

Embody

Bill Stumpf and Jeff Weber
Herman Miller, USA
2009

The backrest is composed of upholstery over a skin of perforated flexing plastic that flexes on a series of armatures connected to a central spine. The seat cushion is constructed with a series of plastic spring coils.

Backrest p103, Seat p166

i2i

Thomas Overthun and IDEO with Steelcase Design Studio
Steelcase, USA
2009

The plastic backrest is perforated with vertical slots, which
make it flexible, and its height forms a ledge that supports
a sitter's arm. The chair was designed for collaborative
work environments.

Backrest p103

ON

Wiege
Wilkhahn, Germany
2009

The backrest is held by the armrest brackets, which allow the
backrest and seat to tilt sideways under a sitter's weight.

Backrest p122, Seat-Stem Joinery p170, Movement p209

Setu

Studio 7.5
Herman Miller, USA
2009

The backrest and seat are constructed with mesh stretched
between flexible, bilateral plastic spines. The weight of a sitter
opens the spines, raises the seat and controls the recline.

Backrest p122

Generation

Formway
Knoll, USA
2009

The backrest is a flexible plastic skin that is electromagnetically welded to an upper and lower frame of rigid plastic. The frames are connected by a central spine which allows the upper-frame to flex behind the sitter's shoulders. The uppermost portion of the backrest bends backward under the weight of a sitter's arm to provide a makeshift armrest.

Backrest pp107, 123, Seat p163, Seat-Stem Joinery p177

Taxonomy

Headrest

Headrests are fairly uncommon features in office chairs, and tend to be employed either to distinguish a chair as executive seating or for ergonomic purposes. This chapter illustrates the various cushioning techniques used in headrests and the supporting structures that have been used to construct them. As the headrest appears infrequently in the history of the office chair it has evolved through only a small number of designs. At times the structural elements of the headrest are used in conjunction with movement or adjustment mechanisms, and this is indicated whenever relevant.

1849

The front face of a wooden panel is covered with batting and velvet. This upholstery approach is centuries old, and an economical way of achieving basic comfort.
Centripetal Spring Armchair, p29

1978

The front face of a moulded-plywood panel is covered with a foam cushion and leather. These materials were unoriginal in their time but had not previously been applied to a headrest.
Fysio, p48

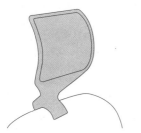

1998

The front face of an injection-moulded glass-reinforced polyamide panel is covered with a Technogel cushion. Similar gels are used for increasing the comfort of modern bicycle seats.
Meda2, p63

1998

A soft, hollow and backless pouf made with injection-moulded Thermolast K TPE is supported by an elliptical injection-moulded plastic frame and covered with a mesh net. This membrane is highly flexible and translucent.
Ypsilon, p64

Suspended Surface

1994

Upholstery is suspended over an injection-moulded polyamide and glass frame. Such a frame was novel and economical, and had not previously been applied to headrests.
Modus, p60

2003

Mesh fabric is suspended in a rigid nylon frame. This head-rest employs a construction approach that was originally developed for the backrest and seat of the Aeron Chair.
Xten, p71

1980

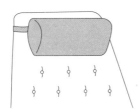

A cushion is strapped to the extended height of the backrest. This feature was adapted from Danish mid-twentieth-century residential lounge chairs.
Milton High, p51

2002

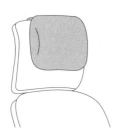

A cushion is sewn as a flap to the height of the upholstered headrest panel. During the first decade of the twenty-first century, lounge-like work environments have gained popularity in corporate environments.
Leap Worklounge, p68

2006

A cushion is attached magnetically to the extended height of the backrest. This design simplifies adjustment, allowing the user to position the cushion freely.
Lotus, p74

Broad Connection to Backrest

1849

The headrest is fixed to a cast-iron lattice attached across the height of the backrest. Elaborate designs such as this were deemed unhygienic in the early twentieth century, as they collect dust and are difficult to clean.
Centripetal Spring Armchair, p29

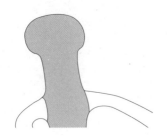

1926

The upholstered wooden backrest panel continues into the headrest. With its anthropomorphic qualities, the headrest resembles many of the primitive objects Freud kept in his office.
Sigmund Freud's Office Chair, p32

1978

A height-adjustable wooden panel is fastened to and overlaps the wooden backrest. The headrest is shaped forward to support the head. Moulded plywood was popularized in domestic furniture in the 1930s, 1940s, and 1950s.
Fysio, p48

2002

The plastic backrest panel continues into the headrest. The headrest pushes forward, like that of the Fysio, but the plastic used here is a cost-efficient alternative to moulded plywood.
Solis, p69

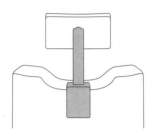

1930s

The headrest is bolted to a machined-aluminium spine that passes through a bracket bolted to the upper backrest. The height is adjustable and the simple structure is easy to clean.
Custom Adjustable Chair, p35

1984

The headrest is held by a depth- and height-adjustable steel tube that extends from a tilting steel-tube backrest spine. The spine's length gives it great flexibility under the weight of the sitter's head.
Capisco, p52

1998

A central plastic clip, moulded with the headrest, is attached to the backrest. This is an economical way of providing an optional headrest.
Meda2, p63

2004

The headrest is mounted to an aluminium extrusion behind the backrest mesh. This is an unconventional and unique construction approach.
H09, p71

Split Single Spine

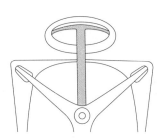

1998

An injection-moulded plastic spine joins the backrest spine to the back of the headrest, allowing it to flex under the weight of the sitter's head.
Ypsilon, p64

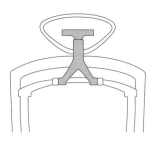

2002

An injection-moulded plastic spine joins the headrest to, and adjusts vertically within, a second spine connected to two points along a crossbar on the backrest.
Contessa, p66

1977

A bilateral steel tube frame is covered with upholstery. This is a typical mid-century furniture construction approach that had not previously been applied to an office chair headrest.
Mister, p47

1994

A bilateral injection-moulded polyamide and glass frame is covered with upholstery. This technique, and the curvature of the headrest, is an advancement on the headrest of the Mister chair of 1977.
Modus, p60

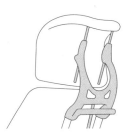

1999

Plastic spines connected to the seat-stem joinery with a steel rod pivot radially within die-cast aluminium spines, tilting the headrest forward as a user reclines. This degree of responsive and supportive headrest movement was highly original.
Freedom, p65

2001

Bilateral injection-moulded plastic hinges allow the headrest to tilt backward independently of the backrest. This is a simple kinetic improvement on the double-spine headrest.
Open Up, p66

2003

The headrest's depth is adjusted as it rotates 360 degrees on injection-moulded plastic bilateral joints. Depth adjustment allows a further degree of accommodation for the user.
Orbit, p70

2003

The headrest is joined to the backrest with fixed bilateral steel profiles. Although this structure had not been applied to an office chair headrest before, it is not any more advanced than the Custom Adjustable Chair of the 1930s.
Solis (second version), p69

2003

The headrest sits on two steel cylinders that penetrate the plastic volume behind the backrest and adjust vertically within it. This adjustment approach is common in automobile headrests.
Xten, p71

2005

The headrest is joined to the backrest panel and supported by a double spine extending from the seat-stem joinery that keeps the headrest upright as the backrest reclines.
Headline, p74

Backrest

Backrests are a key component of the office chair and they have under-gone an extensive evolution. This chapter illustrates the various methods of cushioning and the diverse supporting structures that have been used in backrests. Each cushioning technique has been explored in a seem-ingly endless variation, using a wide spectrum of materials. The structural elements appear in eight morphological variations, and each is shown in several manifestations. At times the structural elements of the backrest are used in conjunction with movement or adjustment mechanisms, and this is indicated whenever relevant.

Panel

1853

The backrest is a plane made from a solid piece of wood. This construction technique is centuries old and was an economical and sturdy solution in the nineteenth century.
Sitting Chair, p28

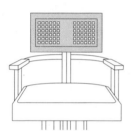

1904

A perforated folded-steel panel is welded at the corners and lacquered. This construction technique was pioneering in its time, and sheet steel became a prominent material used in the office chairs of subsequent decades.
Larkin Building Chair, p31

1938

A moulded, contoured, and perforated panel of Bakelite. Bakelite is considered the first plastic, and colors are inherent to it. Plastics have become fundamental materials used in every contemporary office chair.
Montecatini Headquarters Chair, p35

1953

A moulded, contoured shell of fibreglass and plastic resin. Resin offered brighter colors than any previous plastic, and the added fibreglass provided sufficient strength for this piece to be moulded as a thin shell.
PACC, p37

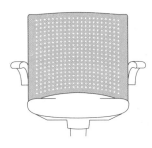

1991

A perforated, contoured, injection-moulded plastic panel.
The injection-moulding process allows this part to be made
with far greater speed and cost efficiency than any previous
plastic backrest panel.
Picto, p58

1996

A moulded, contoured panel of integral polyurethane foam.
Softness and slight flexibility distinguish this material from
other rigid plastics.
Juli, p62

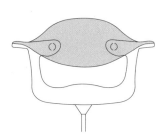

1997

A moulded, contoured panel of opaline. Transparency and
slight flexibility distinguish this material from other plastics.
Spin, p63

1999

A moulded, contoured, and perforated panel of slightly
flexible plastic. This component is similar to the backrest of
the Picto of 1991, but more flexible.
Caper Chair, p64

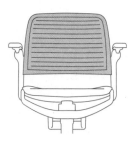

2002

A moulded, contoured, and slotted polypropylene panel. The slots make this design more flexible than previous plastic backrest panels.
Cachet, p66

2003

A moulded, contoured plastic panel is perforated in a pattern that focuses the flexibility and rigidity in the desired areas.
Mirra Chair, p70

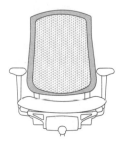

2005

A contoured panel of slightly flexible plastic is moulded in a raised three-dimensional pattern that yields a cushioning effect across the entire panel.
Celle, p72

2006

A translucent, slightly flexible plastic is overmoulded on a less flexible opaque plastic panel. A slit in the lower back allows both materials to flex backward on the bilateral areas of the opaque material.
Otto Chair, p74

1849

Velvet and batting are fixed to a wooden panel with brads. This centuries-old construction technique was an economical solution in the nineteenth century.
Centripetal Spring Armchair, p29

1926

Leather and batting are glued to a narrow wooden panel. This narrow backrest would have allowed Freud to move his upper shoulders freely and made it easier for him to reach items behind him.
Sigmund Freud's Office Chair, p32

1944

Batting and vinyl are glued to a aluminium panel. This highly economical upholstery technique became ubiquitous on the office chairs of subsequent decades.
Steno Posture Chair, p35

1951

Fabric and moulded neoprene foam are glued to a moulded resin and fibreglass structure. The moulded plastic allowed this upholstered backrest to have more curvature than previous designs.
71 Saarinen Armchair, p36

1953

A heat-pressed hopsack pad is glued to a fibreglass shell, its edges captured with a vinyl band. The vinyl band allows the backside of the backrest to be left un-upholstered.
PACC, p37

1956

A fabric-covered wooden panel is captured by a sand-cast aluminium frame. The chair was produced exclusively for the Price Tower, and sand casting was employed as it did not require high tooling investment.
Price Tower Executive Armchair, p38

1964

A tufted upholstery is secured to a transparent thermoplastic shell (PMMA) with metal snaps. Transparent thermoplastic had not been used in office seating before this design, nor has it been employed since.
D-49, p41

1965

A tufted polyester fibre and high-density foam are captured along the edges of an injection-moulded plastic shell with an extruded aluminium frame.
Pollock Chair, p42

1973

An ABS panel is covered with polyurethane foam and a fabric slipcover, which is fixed through the foam to the ABS with two buttons. The panel is made of a flexible plastic that moves under a sitter's recline.
Morrison / Hannah Task Chair, p44

1974

Two self-skinning polyurethane cushions are glued into two separate plastic shells. The cushion surface can be cleaned with a damp cloth and is soft to the touch.
Vertebra, p44

1976

Stretch fabric is glued to three vertically divided cold-moulded polyurethane foam cushions. The separate cushions are intended to provide support to the sides and middle of the back.
238 / 7, p46

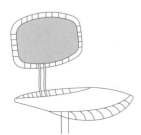

1976

A leather pad is secured over a grid of steel rods that collectively form a supporting surface.
Beaubourg, p46

1976

Stretch fabric is glued to a cold-moulded polyurethane foam cushion glued to a plywood panel. The back is covered with a plastic cap. This construction technique has been emulated by countless subsequent office chairs.
Ergon, p46

1976

The polyurethane foam is moulded directly onto the fabric, quickening the production process.
Vitramat, p49

1977

Fabric is glued around a moulded-foam cylinder that acts as a backrest-armrest. This cylinder rotates around an ovoid, allowing the user to adjust the depth of the backrest.
Rollback Chair, p47

1979

Stretch fabric is glued to a cold-moulded polyurethane foam cushion that is glued to a stamped-steel shell. Borrowed from auto-body production, stamping steel is a highly economical and structural production technique.
Diffrient Advanced Management, p48

1980

Stretch fabric is glued onto a cold-moulded polyurethane foam cushion that is glued to a two-part flexible plastic panel.
454 Concentrx, p50

1984

Stretch fabric is glued to a cold-moulded polyurethane foam cushion with integrated female snap fittings, which attach to male fittings that are spin-welded to a flexible Rynite shell.
Equa Chair, p57

1984

A fabric band is wrapped around an upholstered cold-moulded polyurethane cushion and supporting plastic panel.
Figura, p54

1984

A die-cast aluminium tilt mechanism is placed between the cold-moulded polyurethane foam cushion and a flexible plastic panel. This panel hides the mechanism, making the chair appear less machine-like.
Persona, p55

1987

Stretch fabric is glued to a cold-moulded polyurethane foam cushion, which is glued to a visually distinctive folded-steel panel.
Kite, p56

1989

The upholstered cushions are split horizontally, giving distinct support to the lower and upper backrest.
Hollington Chair, p58

1991

A spring-loaded flexing mechanism is placed between a plastic panel and upholstery, and the entire backrest is covered in segmented leather strips, which are sewn onto and separated by strips of stretch fabric.
Vertair, p59

1992

Two separate upholstered panels move up and down to provide a range of back support. This backrest was designed to provide support to the sacral region of the back and to allow a seated person to adjust support correctly for his or her body size.
Zackback, p59

1994

The fabric covering the backrest is a three-dimensional knit that stays on tightly without the use of glue. This technology allows a piece of fabric to be knitted with integral contour, and it is used on several subsequent backrests.
T Chair, p60

1996

A large flap of fabric is sewn to the reverse of the upholstered cushion, allowing it to slip over the plastic backrest.
Axess, p62

1999

A polypropylene panel with a slotted lower portion can be adjusted by turning a knob, which alters its depth and curvature.
Leap, p65

2003

Two upholstered plastic panels are mounted on a rigid frame. These independent panels flex under the weight of a seated person's shoulders.
Duo Back, p69

2003

A moulded, contoured plastic panel is perforated and covered in fabric. The perforated pattern focuses flexibility and rigidity in the desired areas of the backrest.
Mirra Chair, p70

2006

A flexible, contoured Hytrel panel is mounted on a rigid frame and covered with an electro-welded fabric. The upper left and right areas of the backrest flex under the weight of a seated person's shoulders.
Sguig, p75

2009

A steel frame is overmoulded with a semi-rigid self-skinning polyurethane foam. This element may be used as a backrest or armrest.
360°, p77

2009

The flexing backrest panel has vertical slots cut from its surface and ends with a soft band at the top. The front face of the panel is covered with a mesh fabric. The soft band flexes under the weight of a seated person's arms.
Cobi, p77

2009

Mesh upholstery covers a skin of perforated plastic, which is connected to a series of plastic armatures attached to a central spine. Each of these armatures flexes under a seated person's weight, creating a high degree of support.
Embody, p77

2009

The plastic backrest is perforated with vertical slots, which make it flexible, and a ledge at its height supports a sitter's arm. The chair was designed for collaborative, lounge-like work environments.
i2i, p78

Suspended Surface

1865

Woven rattan is held in a closed bentwood frame. This technique allows breathability and transparency, and inspired future generations of suspended backrests, including that of the Aeron Chair.
Revolving Armchair, p28

1928

Sewn leather is stretched between bilateral steel tubes. The use of steel tubes in furniture production was popularized in the 1920s and 1930s and remains common today.
B7a, p33

1958

Sewn fabric is held between bilateral die-cast aluminium spines and spread with a die-cast aluminium handle on the backrest and four steel bars in the seat-stem joinery. This was originally designed as outdoor furniture, but was repurposed for the office.
Aluminum Group Chair, p39

1969

Sewn fabric is held between bilateral die-cast aluminium spines and spread with a die-cast aluminium handle on the backrest and four steel bars in the seat-stem joinery. Cushions are sewn onto the suspended fabric.
Aluminum Group Chair (Soft Pad Group), p39

1970

A rubber membrane is suspended in a steel-tube frame with springs. An upholstered slip-on fabric cover is placed over the entire structure. Even though the rubber is hidden, this construction is the first truly elastic suspended backrest.
Light, p43

1973

Fabric is stretched over a steel-tube armrest-backrest frame and fastened to the seat bottom. This distinct structure drew inspiration from tent construction.
Archizoom Uno, p44

1990

Woven rattan is suspended between die-cast aluminium spines. This bumpy surface was inspired by the beaded seat covers found in New York City taxis.
AC 2, p58

1994

An injection-moulded glass-reinforced nylon frame is moulded over suspended mesh made of woven plastic and fabric strands. This technique was subsequently adopted by almost every other manufacturer in the office-seating industry.
Aeron Chair, p61

1998

A panel of flexible semi-transparent TPE plastic is suspended between two points at the top corners of the backrest and at the sides of the lower backrest. The design is inspired by ships' sails, which are held at their extremities.
Ypsilon, p64

2000

Soft polyurethane foam is moulded over a flexing internal steel frame. The design is water-resistant and easily cleaned.
.04, p67

2002

Three pieces of mesh fabric are sewn together along contoured seams that sculpt the fabric in the frame to support the lower back.
Liberty, p68

2004

Mesh is captured and suspended between upper and lower horizontal moulded-plastic supports which are spread by a central spine. The fabric is unsupported along its sides, allowing a seated person to move his or her shoulders freely.
H09, p71

2004

Contoured flexing steel rods across the backrest are held in tension between bilateral plastic spines. Fabric is suspended over the front of the rods. The steel rods provide additional back support and were designed to disassemble easily for recycling.
Think, p73

2007

Suspended lengths of plastic are suspended across the backrest between the bilateral plastic spines. Ratchets adjust the depth of the plastic lengths and control the depth and curvature of the backrest.
Cpod, p76

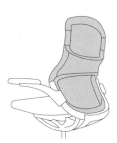

2009

A soft, flexible, and perforated moulded-plastic skin is electromagnetically adhered to a stiffer flexing frame. The upper region of the suspended backrest bends backward to form a makeshift armrest.
Generation, p79

Broad Connection to Seat

1953

The backrest and seat are part of a continuous fibreglass and plastic resin structure. This material and the depth of curvature between the backrest and seat give this component a high degree of structural integrity.
PSCC (armless version of PACC), p37

1955

The backrest and seat are part of a continuous moulded plywood structure. Moulded plywood offers slight flexibility between the backrest and seat.
Model 3107, p36

1965

The backrest and seat are part of a continuous injection-moulded plastic structure, the edges of which are captured in an extruded-aluminium profile. The aluminium profile adds structural integrity to the thin plastic element.
Pollock Chair, p42

1979

The backrest and seat are part of a continuous stamped-steel structure. Stamped steel is a highly economical and structural production technique borrowed from auto-body production.
Diffrient Advanced Management, p48

1979

The backrest is joined across the seat back with a spring-loaded die-cast aluminium joint that allows the backrest to pivot backward.
Supporto, p50

1986

The backrest and seat are joined by a flexing steel spine that is placed between a continuous plastic panel and continuous upholstery.
Sensor, p55

1991

The backrest and seat are joined by a spring-loaded flexing mechanism that is placed between a plastic panel and upholstery.
Vertair, p59

1996

The backrest and seat are part of a continuous soft and slightly flexible integral polyurethane foam structure.
Juli, p62

2003

The backrest and seat are part of a continuous injection-moulded polypropylene structure. This production technique is more cost- and time-efficient than the moulded fibreglass used in the PACC of 1958.
Spoon Chair, p71

1953

The backrest, armrests, and seat are part of a continuous fibreglass and plastic-resin structure. This material and the depth of curvature between the features give this component a high degree of structural integrity.
PACC, p37

1980

The backrest, armrest and seat are part of a continuous steel-tube structure which is covered with foam and leather. These were common materials at the time, but the structural configuration was novel.
Milton High, p51

1989

The backrest and armrests are part of the same injection-moulded plastic structure, and are joined to the seat.
Hollington Chair, p58

1994

The backrest and armrests are part of the same leather and steel structure and are joined to the seat. This production technique was inspired by the construction of riding saddles.
Incisa, p59

Single Spine

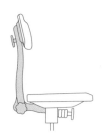

1885

The angle of the wooden spine that holds the backrest is adjustable with a knob at its bottom. The angle of the backrest panel is adjusted with a second knob that pierces the upper spine.
Unknown 2, p30

1925

A formed steel bar joins the seat and backrest. Formed steel bars are still used as office chair spines.
Unknown 3, p31

1973

The angle of the injection-moulded ABS spine that holds the backrest is adjustable with a knob at its bottom. The angle of the backrest panel is adjusted with a second knob that connects it to the upper spine.
Synthesis 45, p45

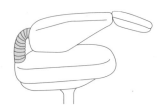

1976

The spine bends forward, allowing the backrest to lie on top of the seat for compact storage or shipping.
238/7, p46

1976

The broad spine is covered in upholstery, and meets the backrest on a pivoting joint at mid-backrest.
Vitramat, p49

1977

A bent steel-tube spine supports an upholstered cylindrical backrest-armrest. This cylinder rotates around an ovoid, allowing the user to adjust the depth of the backrest.
Rollback Chair, p47

1980

A steel spine is mounted on a 30-degree angle that allows the depth and height of the backrest to be adjusted with one motion.
Diffrient Basic Operational Chair, p51

1980

A steel spine joins the upholstered backrest to the underside of the seat, where a knob controls the depth of the backrest.
Stephens High Back Executive Chair, p51

2003

The plastic spine pivots forward allowing the backrest to lie on top of the seat for compact storage or shipping.
Giroflex 63, p70

2004

A pivoting joint at the top of the spine tilts an upholstered panel from a vertical to a horizontal position, transforming it from a backrest to an armrest.
Tacit, p72

2006

A rigid Hytrel spine diverges and converges around the lower back and rises along the upper back as a single spine. This structure supports a soft backrest panel, and allows the upper left and right areas of the panel to flex.
Sguig, p75

1956

A sand-cast aluminium split spine connects the backrest frame to the seat-stem joinery. The chair was produced exclusively for the Price Tower, and sand casting was employed as it did not require a large investment in tooling.
Price Tower Executive Armchair, p38

1950s

An extruded-aluminium spine is attached to the seat-stem joinery on a single adjustable pivoting joint. The spine is attached to two diverging spines made of aluminium bar, which attach to the backrest on pivoting joints.
Unknown 4, p41

1976

An extruded steel spine is attached to a tilting mechanism under the seat. A second spine adjusts vertically within the first spine, and is welded to a diverging steel plate attached to the backrest.
Ergon, p46

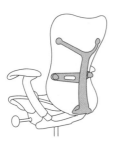

2003

An injection-moulded plastic split spine is connected to the tilting mechanism under the seat. The spine is fixed to the uppermost corners of the backrest, and a plastic lumbar support panel attaches it to the sides of the mid-backrest.
Mirra Chair, p70

Single Spine with Armrest Connection

1904

The backrest pivots on a central steel spine welded to curved steel lengths that continue into the armrests. Sheet steel became a prominent material used in the office chairs of subsequent decades and is still used today.
Larkin Building Chair, p31

1926

The wooden upholstered backrest continues into the armrests and seat. This contributes to the anthropomorphic quality of the chair.
Sigmund Freud's Office Chair, p32

1955

The backrest is held by a central steel tube and a continuous wooden backrest-armrest structure that is milled with ergonomic contours.
PP 502, p38

1956

A sand-cast aluminium spine and armrests hold the backrest. The spine is attached to the base.
Price Tower Armchair, p38

1976

The backrest is held by a steel tube and a continuous upholstered moulded-plastic armrest-backrest structure. The use of
plastic on this structure is a technical advance on the wooden
armrest-backrest structure of the 1955 PP 502.
MKD, p47

1988

The backrest is held by the sub-seat mechanism and armrests.
Acting as a pivoting member between its supporting elements,
the backrest assists the synchronized recline between the
backrest and seat.
AC 1, p56

1995

The backrest is held by a central spine and arms, all made
of injection-moulded nylon. An upholstered cushion is placed
onto this structure.
Avian Work Chair, p62

Double Spine

1872

A cast-iron double spine holds the wooden backrest and tilts from a spring-loaded joint under the seat.
Unknown 1, p30

1929

The backrest pivots on and is supported by bilateral wooden spines attached to the sides of the seat.
Drehstuhl, p32

1938

The backrest is supported by bilateral square aluminium lengths attached to the seat back.
Montecatini Headquarters Chair, p35

1944

Two square aluminium tubes, bent from the same length, hold the backrest panel on pivoting joints. This structure is attached to a pivoting mechanism under the seat.
Steno Posture Chair, p35

1958

A piece of fabric that forms the backrest and seat is suspended in bilateral die-cast aluminium spines which are spread by a die-cast aluminium handle on the backrest and four steel bars in the seat-stem joinery.
Aluminum Group Chair, p39

1970

The upholstered plastic backrest pivots on bilateral joints to the seat.
232, p43

1978

The backrest is supported by bilateral internal rolled-steel frames which are joined to each other with welded cross-brackets and covered in leather. This production technique was taken from the automotive bumper industry.
Sapper Chair, p48

1982

The backrest is supported by forward cantilevering, bilateral injection-moulded plastic armrests.
Kevi 2, p52

1983

The injection-moulded plastic backrest is attached to a lower backrest that continues from the seat with bilateral spring-loaded joints covered in rubber bellows.
Dorsal, p52

1984

An injection-moulded Rynite backrest is a continuous element with bilateral flexing spines and the seat. The flexing spines provide additional recline to that given by the mechanism under the seat.
Equa Chair, p57

1992

Two steel tubes, bent from the same length, support two height-adjustable upholstered backrest panels that slide vertically along the tubes.
Zackback, p59

1994

The backrest is supported by bilateral aluminium spines that join the backrest to the movement mechanism in the seat-stem joinery.
Aeron Chair, p61

1998

Two backrest panels are connected to bilateral steel spines at pivoting joints.
Tris, p64

2000

The backrest is supported by bilateral internal flexing steel slats which are overmoulded with self-skinning polyurethane foam.
.04, p67

2002

Bilateral flexing steel-rod spines coil under the seat. The coils provide spring as a sitter reclines.
Perpetual 4300 Series, p69

2003

Bilateral spines merge into a single horizontal support, which holds two backrest panels on pivoting joints.
Duo Back, p69

2005

The backrest is supported by a die-cast aluminium double spine with hinged connections to the lower backrest and headrest.
Headline, p74

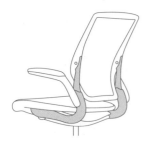

2008

The backrest is supported by and pivots on bilateral backrest spines, which rest and pivot on a plastic bracket attached to the stem.
Diffrient World, p76

2009

Die-cast aluminium spines continue from the armrest supports and hold the backrest at pivoting joints that allow the seat and backrest to shift sideways under a sitter's weight.
ON, p78

2009

Bilateral spines moulded in two densities of flexing plastic are connected by two cross-bars and the seat-stem joinery.
Setu, p78

1853

Eight wooden dowels join the backrest-armrest structure and the seat. This structure was popularized by residential Windsor chairs during the eighteenth century.
Sitting Chair, p28

1897

Six wooden slats join the upper backrest panel to the seat and armrests. The slats provided more surface area for the back than the dowels common to chairs like the 1853 Sitting Chair.
Office Chair No. 982, p31

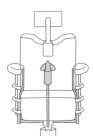

1930s

A height- and angle-adjustable aluminium spine joins the backrest to the seat-stem joinery. Bilateral hinged spines connect the backrest sides to the armrest supports.
Custom Adjustable Chair, p35

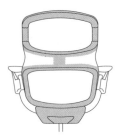

2009

Two injection-moulded plastic spines join the lower backrest to the seat-stem joinery. These continue upward into a loop, which is connected to a second loop by a single spine that allows a seated person's shoulders to flex backward.
Generation, p79

Armrest Connection

1929

The backrest and armrest are part of a continuous structure made of jointed wood, which is covered tightly with batting and leather.
Maharaja, p34

1951

The backrest and armrest are part of a continuous structure made of moulded fibreglass and plastic resin, and covered with sisal, moulded foam and fabric.
71 Saarinen Armchair, p36

1958

The backrest-armrest structure is connected to the raised seat structure by its armrests. Both elements are made with moulded fibreglass and plastic resin.
DAF Chair, p40

1958

The backrest is connected to the armrests with die-cast aluminium arms. The arms are joined to the backrest on articulating ball and socket joints and bolted to the underside of the armrests.
MAA Chair, p40

1970

The backrest is supported by die-cast aluminium armrests that wrap behind the backrest.
Morrison / Hannah Task Chair, p44

1974

The backrest is attached to and flexes backward on steel-tube armrests covered in rubber bellows.
Vertebra, p44

1984

The upholstered plastic backrest is supported by pivoting joints to the armrests, which allows the backrest to tilt backward.
Helena, p54

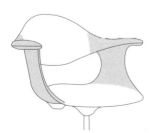

1997

The opaline backrest is mounted to a raised polypropylene seat-armrest structure. The entire structure flexes slightly.
Spin, p63

1998

The injection-moulded plastic backrest is joined to the armrests with integrated bilateral sockets that fit on to the armrest posts.
Caper Chair, p64

1999

The backrest pivots on joints to the armrests that can be adjusted to different degrees of tension with a knob.
Leap, p65

Armrest

Armrests appear on most office chairs and they have undergone an extensive evolution. This chapter illustrates the various cushioning techniques and supporting structures that have been used to construct armrests. Armrests are generally located close to the seat, backrest and seat-stem joinery, so there are many ways in which they can be attached to the chair. In some cases they have even been used as a structural element to support the backrest. At times the structural elements of the armrest are used in conjunction with a movement mechanism, and this is indicated when necessary. Armrest height, depth and span adjustment are described whenever relevant.

Panel

1853

A wooden plane cut with a contoured shape. This centuries-old construction technique was an economical and sturdy solution in the nineteenth century.
Sitting Chair, p28

1904

A folded and welded steel sheet finished with lacquer. This was a pioneering construction technique in its time, and sheet steel became a prominent material used in the office chairs of subsequent decades.
Larkin Building Chair, p31

1953

A moulded, contoured shell of fibreglass and plastic resin. Resin offered brighter colors than any previous plastic, and the added fibreglass provided sufficient strength for this piece to be moulded as a thin shell.
PACC, p37

1958

A die-cast aluminium frame. This was the first use of die-cast aluminium for an office chair armrest. This material has been applied to many subsequent armrest structures but tends to be covered with a pad, as it is cold and hard to the touch.
Aluminum Group Chair, p39

1964

A transparent thermoplastic (PMMA) formed sheet. This thermoplastic had not been used in office seating before this design, nor has it been employed since.
D-49, p41

1965

An injection-moulded plastic frame. This design is structurally similar to the Aluminum Group Chair of 1958. This was the first injection-moulded plastic armrest, and the technique has been employed in the production of countless subsequent armrests.
Pollock Chair, p42

1974

A steel tube is covered in rubber bellows. The bellows expand and contract as the steel tube armrest flexes. This technique had not been utilized in office seating before, nor has it been used since.
Vertebra, p44

1996

A contoured moulded integral polyurethane foam panel flexes under the weight of a user's arm.
Juli, p62

Panel and Upholstery

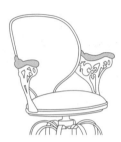

1849

Velvet batting and wood on a cast-iron frame. This centuries-old construction technique was an economical solution in the nineteenth century.
Centripetal Spring Armchair, p29

1926

Leather and batting are glued to a wooden panel. The leather is tightly wrapped around the form, a technique employed by many mid-twentieth-century office chairs.
Sigmund Freud's Office Chair, p32

1930s

Vinyl and batting are glued to a wooden panel. Vinyl and similar synthetic fabrics were utilized to the point of ubiquity by subsequent mid-twentieth-century office chairs.
Custom Adjustable Chair, p35

1953

A heat-pressed hopsack pad is glued to a contoured fibre-glass shell and captured along its edges with a plastic band.
PACC, p37

1989

Leather and polyurethane foam are glued to an injection-moulded contoured plastic panel.
Hollington Chair, p58

1999

Fabric over a gel pad on an injection-moulded plastic structure. The use of gel padding was inspired by bicycle seats.
Freedom, p65

2009

A steel frame is overmoulded with a semi-rigid self-skinning polyurethane foam. This element may be used as a backrest or armrest.
360°, p77

Broad Connection to Seat

1929

The armrest is made of jointed wood, which is covered tightly with batting and leather, and joined across the side of the seat.
Maharaja, p34

1951

The contoured moulded-fibreglass and plastic resin armrest is covered in upholstery and joined to the underside of the seat.
71 Saarinen Armchair, p36

1951

The contoured moulded-fibreglass and resin armrest is covered in upholstery and joined across the side of the seat.
Flying Duck Chair, p36

1958

The armrest-backrest is a continuous moulded fibreglass and resin shell that is held by a second shell of the same material, which continues from the seat.
DAF Chair, p40

1958

The armrest and seat are part of a continuous moulded fibre-glass and resin shell.
MAA, p40

1964

The armrest is a formed sheet of transparent thermoplastic (PMMA) held by a second formed sheet that continues from the seat. This material had not been used in office seating before this design, nor has it been employed since.
D-49, p41

1996

The armrest and seat are part of a continuous soft integral polyurethane shell that flexes under the weight of a sitter's arm.
Juli, p62

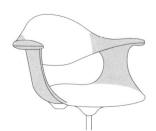

1997

The armrest-backrest is a continuous moulded-opaline shell fastened to a second shell of polypropylene that continues from the seat. The opaline shell is slightly flexible and translucent.
Spin, p63

2006

Upholstery covers a folding internal mechanism that flops over the side of the chair, allowing a user to sit sideways.
Permiso, p75

2006

Stretch three-dimensional knitted fabric conceals an internal mechanism that allows the armrest to adjust vertically, and continues from the armrest into the seat.
Worknest, p76

1953

The armrests, backrest, and seat are part of a continuous fibreglass and plastic resin structure. These materials and the depth of curvature between the backrest and seat give this component a high degree of structural integrity.
PACC, p37

1980

The armrests, backrest and seat are part of a continuous steel-tube structure which is covered with foam and leather. These were common materials at the time, but the structural configuration was novel.
Milton High, p51

1989

The armrest and backrest are a single injection-moulded plastic structure and are joined to the seat.
Hollington Chair, p58

1994

The armrest and backrest are a single structure of steel and leather, and are joined to the seat. This production technique was inspire by riding-saddle construction.
Incisa, p59

Single Connection to Backrest

1978

Injection-moulded glass-reinforced plastic armrests are bolted along the backrest and the side of the seat in three places. The strength of the material and long overlap with the backrest and seat give the armrests structural integrity.
Sapper Chair, p48

1984

Upholstered plastic armrests continue from the backrest. These small and soft armrests are intended to allow the user to easily adopt informal positions and even sit in the chair backward.
Capisco, p52

1994

The armrests pivot horizontally on die-cast aluminium supports, which are joined to the side of the die-cast aluminium backrest structure. The armrests' height can be adjusted along a track on the backrest structure.
Aeron Chair, p61

2002

The armrests are held by a length of curved die-cast aluminium that supports the backrest and is attached under the seat.
Liberty, p68

2003

The armrests are held by a single die-cast aluminium support that continues behind the backrest and intersects the backrest's spine.
Orbit, p70

2003

Injection-moulded plastic armrests continue from the backrest. A large curved transition between the two elements provides sufficient strength for the material's thickness to be kept to a minimum.
Spoon Chair, p71

2003

The armrests are held by a single injection-moulded plastic support that continues behind, and adjusts vertically along, the plastic volume supporting the backrest.
Xten, p71

Single Connection to Backrest with Posts

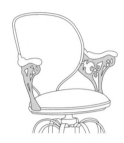

1849

A cast-iron lattice connects each armrest to the middle of the backrest and the sides of the seat. Intricate structures collect dust and are not easily cleaned. Iron is heavier than the plastic or aluminium used in twentieth-century office chairs.
Centripetal Spring Armchair, p29

1865

The armrest is a circular bentwood profile that connects the upper backrest to the underside of the front of the seat. Thonet's bentwood construction was highly economical and efficient in its time.
Revolving Armchair, p28

1897

The armrest is a wooden slat that continues from the backrest, bends under itself, and connects to the seat. Three wooden dowels join the underside of the armrest to the seat. This construction drew from Windsor chairs.
Office Chair No. 982, p31

1904

Made of folded and welded sheet steel, the armrests are bolted to the backrest spine and welded to a steel post attached to the side of the seat.
Larkin Building Chair, p31

1926

A leather-covered wooden armrest is joined to the wooden backrest and a wooden post attached to the seat.
Sigmund Freud's Office Chair, p32

1928

A bent-steel tube is bolted to the backrest and to the side of the seat. The use of steel tubes in furniture production was popularized in the 1920s and 1930s and remains common today.
B7a, p33

1955

A milled wooden armrest continues from the backrest and is intersected by a steel tube that is connected to the seat. This armrest was originally produced using a copy lathe.
PP 502, p38

1956

A sand-cast aluminium armrest is bolted to a backrest frame and post of the same material. The chair was produced exclusively for the Price Tower, and sand casting was employed as it did not require high tooling investment.
Price Tower Armchair, p38

1974

The armrest is a steel tube that joins the rear of the seat to the middle of the backrest, and flexes under the weight of a seated person's recline. This steel tube is covered with flexible rubber bellows.
Vertebra, p44

1976

The armrest is an upholstered panel of injection-moulded plastic bolted to a length of aluminium that joins it to the underside of the seat. This design references the PP 502 of 1955, updating it with plastic.
MKD, p47

1979

The armrest is attached to the middle of the backrest with a pivoting joint that tilts the upper backrest forward to support the seated person's shoulders under the weight of his or her recline.
Diffrient Executive Highback, p50

1980

The armrest is attached at the backrest and the side of the seat on pivoting joints, and the vertex of the armrest flexes as a sitter reclines. These pivoting and flexing points form part of the chair's synchronized reclining mechanism.
FS Chair, p53

1984

The armrest is attached to two metal vertical lengths on pivoting joints. These vertical lengths pivot at their joints to the side of the seat, and form part of the chair's synchronized movement reclining mechanism.
System 25, p55

1988

The armrests are joined behind the backrest on a pivoting length. The armrest is also attached to the underside of the seat on a pivoting joint. These pivoting joints form part of the chair's synchronized reclining mechanism.
AC 1, p56

Double Connection to Backrest

1937

Two steel profiles welded to the backrest frame support wooden armrests. These were the first forward-cantilevered armrests.
S.C. Johnson & Son Building Armchair, p34

1994

A single piece of injection-moulded nylon forms the armrest and its supporting length. The ends of each are bolted to the backrest frame.
Modus, p60

1999

Two steel lengths pivot at their joints to the armrest and backrest frame, allowing the height of the armrests to be adjusted.
Freedom, p65

1977

A bent steel-tube spine supports an upholstered cylindrical backrest-armrest. This cylinder rotates around an ovoid, allowing the user to adjust the depth of the backrest.
Rollback Chair, p47

1978

A die-cast aluminium post supports a moulded polyurethane foam armrest and adjusts vertically within a second die-cast aluminium post that is attached under the seat. Height adjustment is now a standard feature of armrests.
Kevi (height-adjustable version), p40

1980

A die-cast aluminium post fixed under the seat continues into a forward-cantilevered armrest. Like those of the S.C. Johnson & Son Building Armchair of 1937, the armrests are not supported at the sides of the seat and leave room for a user to shift his or her legs to the side.
454 ConCentrx, p50

1980

The steel armrest post houses a cable that triggers seat height-adjustment from a button under the armrest.
Diffrient Basic Operational Chair, p51

1980

A steel bar joins the upholstered armrests to the underside of the seat, where a knob controls the span of the armrests.
Stephens High Back Executive, p51

1983

A bent steel-tube post is attached under the seat, and cantilevers backward to support a moulded-plastic armrest panel.
Dorsal, p52

1984

An injection-moulded plastic post cantilevers backward into an armrest panel and adjusts vertically over a steel-tube post that is attached under the seat. A knob at the bottom of the plastic post controls its height.
Credo, p54

1984

A bent-steel tube, attached under the seat on a pivoting joint, cantilevers backward to hold an armrest pad and connects to the backrest on a second pivoting joint. These pivoting joints allow the backrest to tilt backward.
Helena Chair, p54

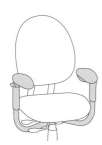

1989

Injection-moulded plastic armrests and supporting posts spread apart simultaneously to accommodate varying body widths.
Criterion, p56

1991

An injection-moulded plastic post is attached under the seat and cantilevers backward to form the armrest.
Vertair, p59

1994

An injection-moulded plastic post supports a plastic and poly-urethane armrest pad that rotates 180 degrees and adjusts vertically over a die-cast aluminium post attached under the seat.
T Chair, p60

1998

A die-cast aluminium post supports a moulded polyurethane foam armrest at the back and adjusts vertically within an injection-moulded plastic post that passes through the seat-stem joinery.
Meda2, p63

1999

An injection-moulded plastic post supports a plastic panel
and polyurethane foam armrest and allows them to adjust
forward, sideways, and backward.
Leap, p65

2000

An injection-moulded plastic post continues into an armrest
panel and adjusts vertically over a second die-cast aluminium
post attached to a pivoting joint under the seat. This joint allows the armrest to pivot backward out of the sitter's way.
H05, p65

2004

An injection-moulded plastic post is attached to an armrest
made of the same material and polyurethane foam on a pivoting joint that allows the armrest to tilt downward.
H09, p71

1955

A steel tube attached under the seat holds the wooden arm-rest at its end and on a raised steel rod. Because the arm-rests are supported at the back of the sides of the seat, they leave room for a user to shift his or her legs to the side.
Model 3107, p36

2002

An injection-moulded plastic post supports the armrest on two raised points, and fits over and adjusts vertically on a second injection-moulded plastic post.
Contessa, p66

2005

The split lengths of an injection-moulded glass-filled nylon post are screwed to the armrest pad. The post adjusts verti-cally in a ratcheted shaft that is fixed to the side of the seat at two points.
Chadwick, p72

Double Post

1930s

Vertical aluminium tubes support an armrest cushion, are cross-braced with horizontal aluminium tubes, and are welded to the seat frame.
Custom Adjustable Chair, p35

1950s

A continuous die-cast aluminium double post is joined to the side of the seat and supports an armrest pad.
Unknown 4, p41

2000

The plastic armrest is injection-moulded as a continuous element with its supports, which are held by a die-cast aluminium structure under the seat.
.04, p67

1885

A length of bentwood continues from the backrest, connects to the seat, forms the armrest, and is attached to the backrest. Thonet's wood production was the most sophisticated of its time, allowing complex shapes such as this.
Revolving Rocking Armchair, p30

1958

A die-cast loop has three raised points at which it is bolted to the seat frame. This material has been applied to many subsequent armrest structures but tends to be covered with a pad, as it is cold and hard to the touch.
Aluminum Group Chair, p39

1960

A die-cast aluminium loop is integrated with the backrest spine and supports the armrest cushion on two raised points.
Time-Life Chair, p41

1965

An injection-moulded plastic loop is attached to the side of the backrest and seat. This structure is almost identical to that of the Aluminum Group Chair of 1958, but its distinctive plastic was used to achieve a warmer touch.
Pollock Chair, p42

Lumbar Support

Prior to 1994, when the Aeron Chair introduced the independent lumbar support, lower back support was integrated into the curvature of the backrest. For this reason this chapter begins in 1994 when the lower back support became an independent component of the office chair. Lower back support is most commonly referred to as lumbar support. A few chairs provide support to the sacral or thoracic region of the back, and this is indicated whenever relevant. Most lumbar supports are adjustable to some degree, and this has also been noted.

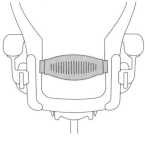

1994

A contoured moulded-polyurethane foam pad can be adjusted vertically, and reversed to vary the depth of the lumbar support. This is the first lumbar support to be made as a separate component from the backrest.
Aeron Chair, p61

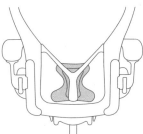

2002

A contoured moulded-polyurethane pad made of three layers supports the sacral area of the back. This was designed as a second, optional lower back support for the Aeron Chair.
Aeron Chair (sacral support version), p61

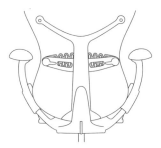

2003

A perforated, contoured, injection-moulded plastic band can be adjusted at varying tensions to increase or decrease the depth of the lumbar support.
Mirra Chair, p70

Panel and Upholstery

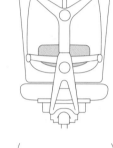

1998

A gel panel is held between the backrest mesh and the suspended backrest surface. The use of gel padding was inspired by bicycle seats.
Ypsilon, p64

2002

A separate pillow is added to the lower backrest. This extra pillow draws from residential lounge chairs. During the first decade of the twenty-first century, lounge-like environments gained popularity in the workplace.
Leap Worklounge, p68

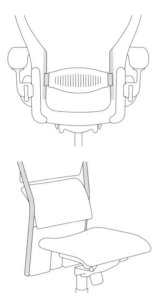

1994

The moulded-polyurethane lumbar support attaches to and adjusts vertically within slots in the sides of the backrest frame. This is the first lumbar support to be made as a separate component from the backrest.
Aeron Chair, p61

1998

An upholstered panel is attached to the double spine of the backrest on pivoting joints. The panel shifts to support the position of a seated person.
Tris, p64

Multiple Connection to Backrest

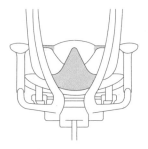

2002

Depth-adjustable bilateral spines, controlled with two knobs, attach the lumbar support panel to the backrest's spines. A supporting panel holds the lumbar support from the bottom of the backrest.
Contessa, p66

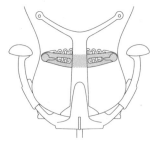

2003

A perforated, contoured, injection-moulded plastic band is attached to the backrest spine and the edges of the backrest panel. The height and depth of the lumbar support is adjusted with two turning levers that hold it to the backrest panel.
Mirra Chair, p70

2007

Suspended lengths of plastic are placed across the backrest and held in tension between the bilateral plastic spines. Ratchets adjust the depth of the plastic lengths and control the depth and curvature of the lumbar area.
Cpod, p76

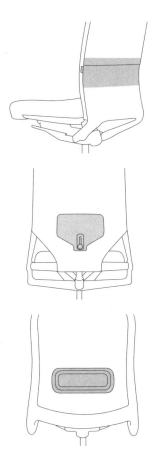

1996

A height-adjustable lumbar support panel is enclosed between the upholstery and the plastic backrest panel. The lumbar support can be adjusted vertically with sliding tabs that protrude from the side of the chair.
Axess, p62

1998

The lumbar support sits between two layers of fabric mesh in the backrest, and is held by a plastic fitting that is clipped over the back layer of mesh.
Meda2, p63

2005

Two pieces of injection-moulded silicone in which magnets are embedded are placed over the front and back of the backrest mesh. These pieces can be moved freely along the backrest and were inspired by magnetic sponges used for cleaning fishtanks.
Chadwick, p72

Seat

Seats are a standard feature of office chairs. Because the seat is supported by the seat-stem joinery, this chapter focuses exclusively on cushioning techniques employed on seats, rather than the supporting structure. An extensive variation of techniques and materials has been used in the cushioning of seats.

1853

The seat is a plane made from a solid piece of wood. This centuries-old construction technique was an economical and sturdy solution in the nineteenth century.
Sitting Chair, p28

1938

A moulded, contoured, and perforated panel of Bakelite. Bakelite is considered the first plastic, and colors are inherent to it. Plastics have become fundamental materials used in every contemporary office chair.
Montecatini Headquarters Chair, p35

1953

A moulded, contoured shell of fibreglass and plastic resin. Resin offered brighter colors than any previous plastic, and the added fibreglass provided sufficient strength for this piece to be moulded as a thin shell.
PACC, p37

1996

A moulded, contoured panel of integral polyurethane foam. Softness and slight flexibility distinguish this material from other rigid plastics.
Juli, p62

1998

A moulded, contoured, and perforated panel of slightly flexible plastic.
Caper Chair, p64

2002

A moulded, contoured, and slotted polypropylene panel. Because of its slots, this design is more flexible than previous plastic seat panels.
Cachet, p66

2005

A moulded, contoured panel of slightly flexible plastic is moulded in a raised three-dimensional pattern that yields a cushioning effect across the entire panel.
Celle, p72

1849

Velvet and batting are fixed to a wooden panel with brads. This centuries-old construction technique was an economical solution in the nineteenth century.
Centripetal Spring Armchair, p29

1944

Batting and vinyl are glued to a steel panel. This highly economical upholstery technique became ubiquitous in subsequent decades.
Steno Posture Chair, p35

1951

Fabric and moulded neoprene foam are glued to a moulded-resin and fibreglass structure.
71 Saarinen Armchair, p36

1953

A heat-pressed hopsack pad is glued to a fibreglass shell and captured along its edges with a plastic band. The band allows the underside of the seat to be left un-upholstered.
PACC, p37

1964

Tufted upholstery is secured to a transparent thermoplastic shell (PMMA) with metal snaps. Thermoplastic had not been used in office seating before this design, nor has it been employed since.
D-49, p41

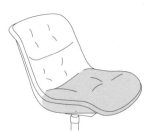

1965

A tufted polyester fibre and high-density foam are captured along the edges of an injection-moulded plastic shell with an extruded-aluminium frame.
Pollock Chair, p42

1973

An ABS panel is covered with polyurethane foam and a fabric slipcover is fixed through the foam to the ABS with two buttons. The panel is made of a flexible plastic that bends under a sitter's weight.
Morrison / Hannah Task Chair, p44

1974

A self-skinning polyurethane cushion is glued onto a plastic shell. The cushion surface can be cleaned with a damp cloth and is soft to the touch.
Vertebra, p44

1976

A leather pad is secured over a grid of steel rods that collectively form a supporting surface.
Beaubourg, p46

1976

Stretch fabric is glued to a cold-moulded polyurethane foam cushion that is glued to a plywood panel. The fabric wraps around the underside of the panel where it is fastened by a plastic cap.
Ergon, p46

1976

Polyurethane foam is moulded directly onto the fabric, which quickens the production process.
Vitramat, p49

1979

Stretch fabric is glued to a cold-moulded polyurethane foam cushion that is glued to a stamped-steel shell. Stamping steel is a highly economical and structural production technique borrowed from auto-body production.
Diffrient Advanced Management, p48

1980

Stretch fabric is glued onto a cold-moulded polyurethane foam cushion that is glued to a two-part plastic panel that flexes forward.
454 ConCentrx, p50

1984

Stretch fabric is glued to a cold-moulded polyurethane foam cushion with integrated female snap fittings, which attach to male fittings that are spin-welded to a flexing Rynite shell.
Equa Chair, p57

1984

Stretch fabric and a cold-moulded polyurethane foam cushion are glued to a plastic panel that flexes downward under the weight of a seated person. The movement mechanism is concealed between these elements in order to make the chair appear less machine-like.
Persona, p55

1987

Stretch fabric is glued to a cold-moulded polyurethane foam cushion, which is glued to a folded-steel panel.
Kite, p56

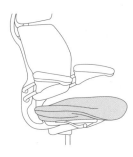

1999

A gel substructure is placed in the cushion.
Freedom, p65

2002

Moulded polyurethane foam is held with fabric to a plastic panel that is perforated to provide specific areas of flexibility.
Life, p68

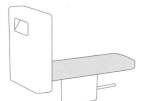

2009

A steel frame is over-moulded with semi-rigid self-skinning polyurethane foam.
360°, p77

2009

Moulded polyurethane foam is held with fabric to a plastic panel that is perforated to provide specific areas of flexibility. This panel sits on the edge of an arching flexible plastic crown that suspends the seat center.
Generation, p79

Suspended Surface

1865

Woven rattan is held in a closed bentwood frame. This technique allows breathability and transparency, and inspired future generations of suspended seats, including that of the Aeron Chair.
Revolving Armchair, p28

1958

Sewn fabric is held between bilateral die-cast aluminium spines and spread with a die-cast aluminium handle on the backrest and four steel bars in the seat-stem joinery.
Aluminum Group Chair, p39

1969

Sewn fabric is held between bilateral die-cast aluminium spines and spread with a die-cast aluminium handle on the backrest and four steel bars in the seat-stem joinery. Cushions are sewn onto the suspended fabric.
Aluminum Group Chair (Soft Pad Group), p39

1970

A rubber membrane is suspended on a steel-tube frame with springs. An upholstered slip-on fabric cover is placed over the entire structure. Even though the rubber is hidden, this construction is the first elastic suspended seat.
Light, p43

1980

A rubber membrane is suspended directly over a steel-tube frame, and an upholstered slip-on fabric cover is placed over the entire structure. This gives the chair a flexible suspended seat, like that of the Light Chair of 1970.
FS Chair, p53

1994

An injection-moulded glass-reinforced nylon frame is moulded over suspended mesh made with woven plastic and fabric strands. This technique was subsequently adopted by almost every other manufacturer in the office-seating industry.
Aeron Chair, p61

1996

The bilateral seat spines suspend the seat front without a cross-bar, which allows the seat front to remain flexible under the weight of a sitter's legs.
Meda Chair, p63

2000

Soft polyurethane foam is moulded over a flexing internal steel frame. The design is water-resistant and easily cleaned.
.04, p67

2003

The front of the frame can be manually adjusted upward or downward with a squeeze handle. This accommodates varying leg lengths.
Mirra Chair, p70

2004

Contoured, flexing steel rods placed across the seat are held between bilateral plastic spines. Fabric is suspended over the rods. The rods provide additional seat support and were designed for easy disassembly for recycling.
Think, p73

2009

A textile is placed over a thin sheet of perforated plastic fixed to a layer of plastic coils. The coils plug into flexible suspended bands that are attached to the sides of the seat frame. These coils were inspired by the coils from spring beds.
Embody, p77

Seat-Stem Joinery

The elements that join the seat and stem of office chairs range from static parts to more complex kinetic mechanisms, which allow the chair to recline. This chapter describes the degree of function carried by the seat-stem joinery and is organized by the number of elements which comprise it. The ten truly unique chair movement methods are described in the movement chapter. These methods and any significant elaborations of them are noted in this chapter. If the seat-stem joinery assists in seat depth adjustment it is also indicated.

Single Connection

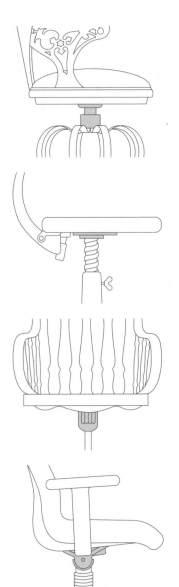

1849

The seat and stem are joined by a wooden central bracket. This centuries-old production technology was an economical and efficient solution in the nineteenth century.
Centripetal Spring Armchair, p29

1872

The seat and stem are joined by a steel plate and bolts. Used for its strength and durability, steel has been an instrumental material in the seat-stem joinery of office chairs since the nineteenth century.
Unknown 1, p30

1897

The seat and stem are joined by a central spring-loaded bracket that allows the seat to tilt backward.
Office Chair No. 982, p31

1979

The seat and stem are joined by a central bracket which is mounted onto a pivoting joint that allows the seat to tilt backward.
Diffrient Advanced Management, p48

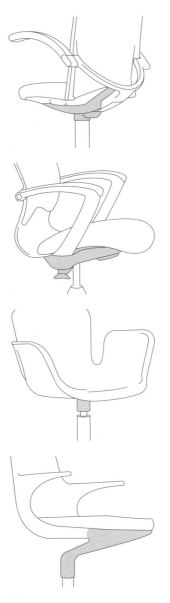

1991

The seat and stem are joined by the housing around the movement mechanism, which holds and moves the seat upward and forward as a sitter reclines.
Picto, p58

1994

The seat and stem are joined by a bracket that allows the seat to slide forward as the backrest reclines on a track.
Soho, p60

1996

The seat and stem are joined by a moulded integral polyurethane socket with an internal steel fitting.
Juli, p62

2003

The front face of the seat is cantilevered forward with a flexible injection-moulded plastic structure that continues into the stem. This gives the seat a slight rearward flex.
Spoon Chair, p71

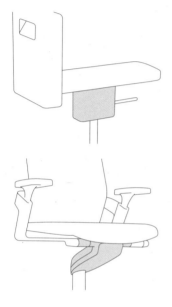

2009

The seat and stem are joined by a steel frame over-moulded with self-skinning polyurethane foam.
360°, p77

2009

The front of the seat and the stem are joined by a die-cast aluminium housing which hosts a tension spring that allows the seat to recline.
ON, p78

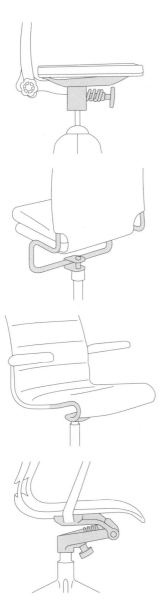

1885

The seat and stem are joined by two folded-steel brackets connected to a folded-steel U-section, which houses a spring-loaded tilt mechanism for the backrest.
Unknown 2, p30

1973

The sides of the seat and the stem are joined by two bent-steel tubes. This production technique was not new in its time, but the structural configuration was. This gives the seat a slight rearward flex.
Archizoom Uno (second version), p44

1977

The front of the seat and the stem are joined by two bent-steel tubes. This production technique was not new in its time, but the structural configuration was. This gives the seat a slight rearward flex.
Mister, p47

1984

The seat is held by two die-cast aluminium arms connected on a pivoting spring-loaded joint to a die-cast aluminium bracket, that cantilevers forward from the stem. The forward-cantilevered pivot lets the user recline and sink from the knees.
Equa Chair, p57

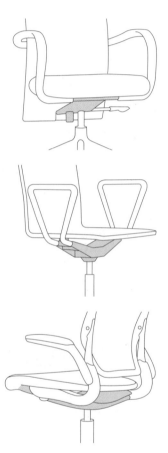

1988

The seat and stem are joined by a die-cast aluminium bracket which is also connected to the bottom of the backrest. Like on the FS Chair of 1980, the seat-stem joinery works with the armrests to allow synchronized seat and backrest recline.
AC 1, p56

2000

The sides of the seat are joined to the stem by a die-cast aluminium bracket. A rubber fitting between the bracket and the stem allows the chair to flex slightly in any direction under a sitter's weight.
.04, p67

2008

The seat is joined to the extended plastic bilateral backrest spines, which rest and pivot on a plastic bracket attached to the stem. Like on the Picto of 1991, the seat-stem joinery lifts the seat as a user reclines against the backrest.
Diffrient World, p76

1937

The seat and stem are joined by three lengths of steel tube. A wing nut placed at the front of the foremost tube can be loosened and tightened to allow the depth of the seat to be adjusted.
S.C. Johnson & Son Building Armchair, p34

1980

The seat and stem are joined by a tilting, spring-loaded, die-cast aluminium bracket and two bilateral spines joined to the backrest and armrests. In conjunction with pivoting armrests, this joinery provides synchronized backrest and seat tilt.
FS Chair, p53

1996

Bilateral seat-backrest spines are joined to the stem by die-cast aluminium arms. A spring-coil shaft joins a rear seat frame to the stem. Pivoting joints on the seat-backrest spines allow the backrest to recline, while the spring limits this motion.
Meda Chair, p63

1998

The front of the seat and the stem are joined with a pivoting, spring-loaded housing, and bilateral armrest spines connect the seat to the stem on a pivoting joint. The joinery provides a similar but less extreme tilt than that of the 1994 Aeron Chair.
Caper Chair, p64

Quadruple Connection

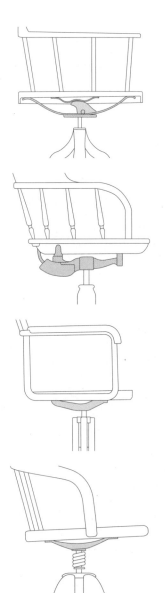

1853

The seat and stem are joined by four flexing steel leaf springs mounted on a steel bar. This joinery allows the seat to tilt backward from its center.
Sitting Chair, p28

1867

Pivoting steel joints attach the sides of the seat to a cast-iron bracket mounted on the stem. An iron rod on the seat rear compresses a spring coil in the iron bracket as a user reclines. A raised point on the bracket stops the seat from tilting forward.
Improved Office Chair, p28

1928

The seat and stem are joined with a cast-aluminium bracket with four arms that splay from the stem.
B7a, p33

1928

The seat and stem are joined by a welded folded-steel bracket with four arms that splay from the stem.
Federdreh, p32

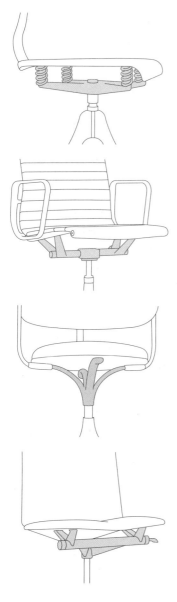

1935

The seat and stem are joined by a folded-steel bracket with four arms that splay from the stem, and steel-spring coils mounted to the ends of each arm. The springs allow the seat to flex and sink slightly in any direction.
Polstergleich, p34

1958

Bilateral seat spines and the stem are joined by four folded sheet steel bars, welded to a pivoting steel tube. The pivot point is located at the center of the seat, allowing a similar rearward tilt to that of the Sitting Chair of 1853.
Aluminum Group Chair, p39

1967

The seat and stem are joined with a die-cast aluminium bracket with four arching arms that splay from the stem.
Model 1904, p43

1987

The seat is held by four folded-steel arms connected on a pivoting, spring-loaded joint to a steel bracket cantilevered forward from the stem. Like the Equa Chair of 1984, the cantilevered pivot point allows a user to recline from the knees.
Kite, p56

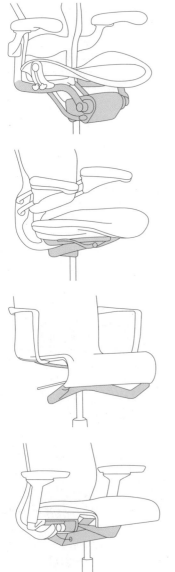

1994

The seat is held by four die-cast aluminium arms connected to two spring-loaded pivot points housed in a container mounted to the stem. The pivot points let the user recline and sink from the ankles.
Aeron Chair, p61

1999

The seat is joined by four hinged arms attached to a bracket mounted on the stem. Like that of the Picto of 1991, the seat-stem joinery lifts the seat as a user reclines against the backrest.
Freedom, p65

2002

At the front, the die-cast aluminium bilateral seat spines curve under themselves and angle inward to join the stem. At the back, the seat spines are joined to the stem by a curved die-cast aluminium bracket.
Rolling Frame, p75

2004

The injection-moulded plastic bilateral seat spines are joined to a bracket mounted to the stem by flexing steel leaf springs. Like that of the Picto of 1991, the seat-stem joinery lifts the seat as the user reclines against the backrest.
Think, p73

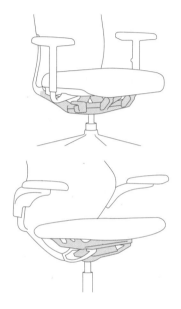

1996

The seat is mounted on four injection-moulded plastic pivoting arms and one spring-loaded fitting that are attached to a die-cast aluminium bracket connected to the stem.
Axess, p62

2009

The plastic seat panel is mounted on a flexible injection-moulded plastic crown, which rests on sliding tracks that allow the seat to be adjusted forward and backward. The tracks are fixed to a plastic and aluminium bracket joined to the stem.
Generation, p79

Stem

The stem connects the base to the rest of the chair and in many cases facilitates the height adjustment of the chair. This chapter illustrates single and multiple stems, describes the various materials used to make them, and the few instances where a new method for height adjustment was introduced. Although all office chairs have a stem, the simplicity of this component has limited the variation in the way it is made. The only example of a multiple stem structure facilitating the movement mechanism is also featured in this chapter.

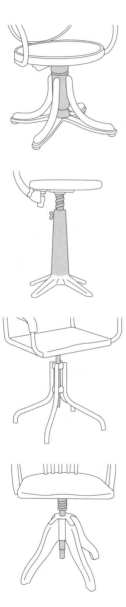

1865

A turned-wood stem holds a swiveling steel post at its height, and is held by the bentwood base legs. Wood turning was a centuries-old technique, but Thonet's bentwood production was the most sophisticated of its time.
Revolving Armchair, p28

1872

A cast-iron stem holds a height-adjustable threaded steel post at its height, which is fixed in place with a wing nut. The stem is continuous with the base. Cast-iron stems were employed on many subsequent nineteenth-century office chairs.
Unknown 1, p30

1928

The legs of the steel-tube base are held together by two steel brackets, which secure the swiveling stem between the legs. The use of steel tubes in furniture production was popularized in the 1920s and the 1930s and remains common today.
B7a, p33

1928

The central joint of the wooden base holds the stem inside a spring, which gives the seat a slight bounce under a sitter's weight. By the 1970s, bounce had become a standard performance of gas-cylinder stems.
Federdreh, p32

1953

A steel post fits into a socket in a die-cast seat-stem joinery bracket, and into a socket in the die-cast aluminium base. The stem is threaded into the base and can be turned to adjust the chair's height.
PACC, p37

1958

Four steel tubes are welded together and continue into the base, where they splay apart and taper into legs.
DAF Chair, p40

1970

A pneumatic cylinder adjusts the seat height when activated by a lever. Prior to this design, chair height was adjusted by rotating the entire chair around a threaded stem. Gas assisted height adjustment is a standard feature of all office chairs today.
232, p43

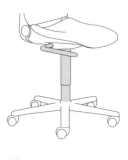

1973

A height-adjustable stem is adjusted by turning a threaded fitting at mid-stem height, and it is concealed by a rubber bellows that adapts its height to the stem. The lower portion of the base is continuous with the injection-moulded ABS base.
Synthesis 45, p45

1849

Eight bent-steel leaf springs connect the seat-stem joinery and base, and allow the seat and backrest to tilt 360 degrees.
Centripetal Spring Armchair, p29

1904

Five cast-iron legs are bolted to the base and seat. The elaborate structure was conceived as a decorative element for the Larkin Building.
Larkin Building Chair, p31

1937

Three steel tubes are welded to the seat-stem joinery and base. Like that of the Larkin Building Chair, this elaborate structure was conceived as a decorative element for the building for which it was designed.
S.C. Johnson & Son Building Armchair, p34

Base

A base is used in all office chair designs and is a defining element of chair construction. This chapter studies platform, triple, quadruple and quintuple base structures, as well as the few instances where footrests have been added to the base. Since the late 1970s, safety regulations in most western countries have demanded a quintuple base of a certain size and strength to ensure stability, and this has curtailed any significant variation in base design. Sextuple bases do exist, but they are excluded from this book, as they are structurally unnecessary and highly uncommon.

1925

A cast-iron pyramidal base with raised corners continues into the stem. Cast iron was an economical and efficient production method in the nineteenth century, but was generally replaced with cast aluminium by the mid-twentieth century.
Unknown 3, p31

1929

A spun-steel circular base and stepped platform are covered with veneer and host the stem. Circular bases were common for chairs that were not placed on casters.
Maharaja, p34

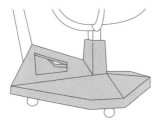

1956

A multifaceted sand-cast aluminium base hosts a central stem, backrest spine and casters. This enormous structure was conceived as a decorative element for the Price Tower.
Price Tower Armchair, p38

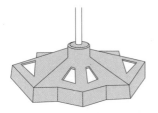

1956

A multifaceted cast-iron base with reliefs on the top facets hosts the stem. Like that of the Price Tower Armchair, this base was conceived as a decorative element for the Price Tower.
Price Tower Executive Armchair, p38

Triple

1965

A three-legged cast-aluminium base hosts the stem and cast-ers. Three-legged bases are notoriously unstable, and have been banned from European and North American offices by safety standards commissions since the 1970s.
FK 6725 Bucket Chair, p42

1937

A length of bent-steel tube welded to a straight length supports a structure of vertical and horizontal steel stems, and hosts three casters.
S.C. Johnson & Son Building Armchair, p34

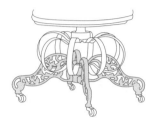

1849

Four cast-iron armatures are connected with a central joint and hold leaf-spring stems and casters. Elaborate designs such as this were deemed unhygienic in the early twentieth century, as they collected dust and were difficult to clean.
Centripetal Spring Armchair, p29

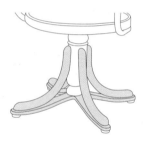

1865

Four bentwood legs are joined to a turned wooden stem and sit on gliders. Thonet's bentwood production was the most sophisticated of its time.
Revolving Armchair, p28

1872

A cast-iron monobloc with four legs forms a continuous structure with the stem. The vast majority of subsequent office chair bases are cast as a single piece.
Unknown 1, p30

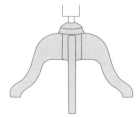

1885

Four wooden legs cut from solid sheets into curved profiles are connected on a central wooden joint that holds the stem. This centuries-old production technology was an economical and sturdy solution in the nineteenth century.
Unknown 2, p30

1928

Four bent steel-tube legs are connected with bolts to cast-aluminium brackets that hold the stem. The use of steel tubes in furniture production was popularized in the 1920s and the 1930s and remains common today.
B7a, p33

1938

A cast-aluminium monobloc with four legs hosts the stem and casters. Cast aluminium is stronger and lighter than iron, and since it was employed for this design it has been used to produce countless office chair bases.
Montecatini Headquarters Chair, p35

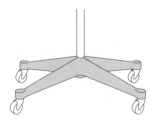

1953

A die-cast aluminium monobloc with four narrow legs and a hollow and ribbed underside hosts the stem. The ends of the base are articulated circles and host the casters.
PACC, p37

1958

Four tapered bent steel-tube legs are welded together at a central point, where they continue into the stem structure. Their bottoms host gliders.
DAF, p40

1966

A folded-steel base with four legs is capped with chromed, scratch-resistant covers. This base was used for several other Knoll chairs, and is still in use today as a quintuple base.
Pearson Executive Chair, p42

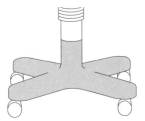

1973

An injection-moulded ABS monobloc with four legs forms a continuous structure with the stem. Plastic is a light and inexpensive alternative to die-cast aluminium and has since become a common base material.
Synthesis 45, p45

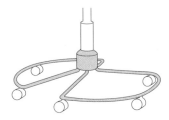

1977

Two sets of two bent-steel legs are formed into loops, and are welded to a central steel cylinder. Six casters are fixed to the underside of the steel-tube loops. This structural configuration is an anomaly.
Mister, p47

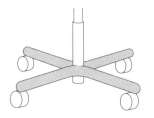

1977

Two bent-steel tubes forming four legs are welded to the central stem, and host casters at their ends.
Rollback Chair, p47

Quadruple with Truss

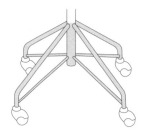

1955

Each of the four legs is constructed of two steel tubes welded to each other at their ends and to the stem.
Model 3107, p36

1955

Each of the four legs is constructed of two steel tubes welded to each other at the midpoint of the upper tube and to the stem.
PP 502, p38

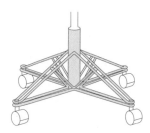

1976

Each of the four legs is constructed of two upper and two lower steel rods, welded to each other at their ends and to the stem. Two additional steel rods are welded to and brace the upper and lower steel rods.
Beaubourg, p46

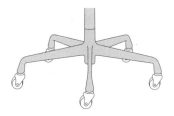

1976

A solid die-cast aluminium monobloc with five legs hosts the stem and casters. The ends of the legs are raised. Quintuple bases are mandated by safety regulations and insurance agencies to protect chairs from tipping over.
Aluminum Group Chair, p39

1979

A die-cast aluminium monobloc with five legs and a hollow and ribbed underside is overmoulded with plastic and hosts the stem and casters. Aluminium is often overmoulded with plastic to make the base resistant to scratching.
Diffrient Advanced Management, p48

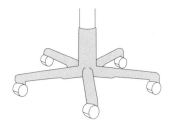

1984

An injection-moulded polypropylene monobloc with five legs forms a continuous structure with the stem and hosts the casters. Plastic is lighter and less expensive than die-cast aluminium.
Persona, p55

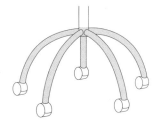

1994

Five bent steel-tube legs are welded to the stem, and their bottoms host gliders. Although steel tubes had been used to make chair bases since the 1930s, none had been made with five legs.
Incisa, p59

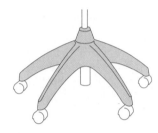

1994

An injection-moulded, glass-reinforced nylon monobloc with five legs hosts the stem and casters. Glass-reinforced nylon has since become a common material used in base production.
Soho, p60

1999

A die-cast aluminium monobloc with five ribbed legs hosts the stem and casters. The ribs add strength and allow the design to remain thin. Similar ribs were employed on die-cast aluminium quadruple bases of the 1940s.
Caper Chair, p64

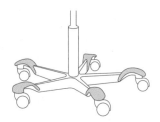

1984

The ends of the die-cast aluminium base form a curved foot-rest, supported from below by an integral structural rib.
Capisco, p52

1984

Scratch-resistant injection-moulded plastic end caps are placed at the end of the die-cast aluminium base.
Credo, p54

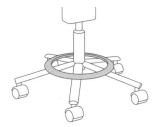

2009

A die-cast aluminium footrest ring rests on top of the five legs of the base.
360°, p77

Floor Contact

Office chairs generally meet the floor with casters, and occasionally with gliders. This chapter examines single casters, double casters and gliders. The single caster was superseded in the 1960s by the double caster, which moves with far greater ease. Steel and cast iron were employed for wheels and gliders up until the 1950s when plastics were introduced. Information on castors or gliders is often excluded from manufacturer or museum catalogues. For this reason, floor contact was one of the most challenging elements of the office chair to study, and the examples featured here came from a small number of resources.

1849

A cast-iron caster is held by a bilateral steel structure and is connected to the base on a joint that rotates 360 degrees. Casters were used on bed frames and other furniture items, but had not previously been integrated into a manufactured chair. *Centripetal Spring Armchair, p29*

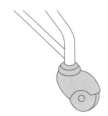

1955

A steel hood shields the upper half of the rubber caster. The hood keeps the rotating wheel from catching on a seated person's foot. *Model 3107, p36*

1958

A rubber caster is held by a bilateral steel structure and connected to the base on a joint that rotates 360 degrees. Rubber and plastics have since become standard caster materials, as they make less noise and cause less damage to floors. *Aluminum Group Chair, p39*

Double Caster

1965

An injection-moulded plastic double caster with a hood.
Double casters move with far greater ease than single casters.
The Kevi caster became an industry standard and has been
used on countless other chairs.
Kevi, p40

1970

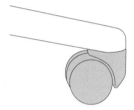

A double caster made with injection-moulded plastic is joined
to the plastic base with a fitting that adheres to the shape of
the base.
232, p43

1988

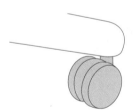

Injection-moulded nylon double casters are joined to the
base with a die-cast aluminium plug.
Ergon, p46

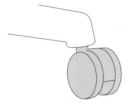

1994

Injection-moulded nylon double casters are joined to the base with an injection-moulded nylon plug. Previously metal plugs were used.
Aeron Chair, p61

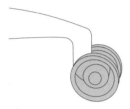

2002

An injection-moulded double caster has transparent plastic disks.
Liberty, p68

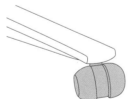

2005

Injection-moulded plastic tapering casters.
Life Chair, p68

Glider

1865

A wooden disk is mounted underneath the end of the base. The glider is employed to reduce damage to the wooden base, and to concentrate the area where the base meets and could potentially scratch the floor.
Revolving Armchair, p28

1930s

An aluminium tube passes through the end of the base and meets the floor with a stepped aluminium disk.
Custom Adjustable Chair, p35

1953

A nylon disk plugs into the ends of the base. Nylon and plastics have since become the standard glider materials, as they cause less damage to floors than gliders made of metal or wood.
PACC, p37

1982

A fixed cylinder is pierced by a tube that plugs into the base.
Kevi 2, p52

1984

A nylon glider 2 inches (5 cm) high, intended for use on hard floors, plugs into the base.
Equa Chair, p57

1988

A stepped nylon and urethane glider 2 inches (5 cm) high plugs into the base.
Ergon, p46

1990

A plastic disk is joined to the base with a steel tube.
AC 2, p58

Methods of Movement

Stem tilts 360 degrees, 1849

The seat and backrest pivot and sink in 360 degrees on eight bent steel leaf springs that connect the seat-stem joinery to the base. This mechanism allows a seated person to lean in any direction, and is the first patented movement mechanism for a desk chair on file. Steel leaf springs were subsequently employed in the vast majority of nineteenth-century movement mechanisms, and are still used in some chairs today, most notably on the Think chair of 2004. However, movement in every direction is not necessarily a desirable feature, as it can make the user feel unstable, and few subsequent chairs have utilized this movement pattern.

Centripetal Spring Armchair, p29

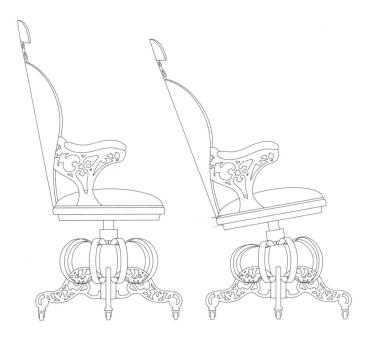

The seat and backrest tilt backward on a central pivot underneath the seat. Two steel leaf springs, which connect the seat front and back to the stem, resist the user's recline and spring the seat into its upright position when the user leans forward. A disadvantage of this method is that the user's feet are lifted from the ground, which gives the impression that it is possible to fall out of the chair backward. Nevertheless, the central pivot was employed on the vast majority of office chairs until more advanced mechanisms were introduced during the 1980s. This proves how little thought went into the movement mechanisms of office chairs during most of the twentieth century, and how far designers' understanding of ergonomics has since developed.

Sitting Chair, p28

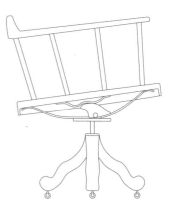

The seat and backrest tilt backward on bilateral pivot points that join the rear of the seat to the seat-stem joinery. A curved steel member protrudes from the rear of the seat and limits its recline by compressing a spring in the seat-stem joinery when the sitter reclines. An arm extends from the seat-stem joinery to provide a platform for the seat front to rest on when it is not in recline. The rear pivot point mechanism lifts the user's feet even further off the ground than the central pivot point mechanism of 1853 and heightens the sensation that one might fall out of the chair backward. It is no wonder that few subsequent chairs employed this movement.

Improved Office Chair, p28

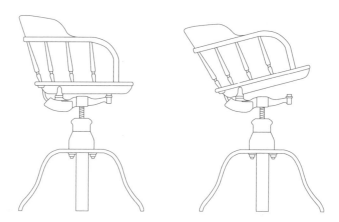

The backrest tilts backward on a spring-loaded pivot point that connects the backrest spine to the underside of the seat. This movement allows a user to recline their back whilst keeping their legs and posterior still. Chairs of this type were popular in factories and telephone operating rooms, but were not commonly used in general business settings, where a greater degree of comfort was expected. This is the first instance of a backrest tilting independently of a seat, a mechanism popularized in the 1980s with advanced movements where the backrest and seat both move, but at varying angles. Tilting spines are also employed in many contemporary office chairs that use advanced methods of backrest and seat recline, such as the Ypsilon of 1998.

Unknown 1, p30

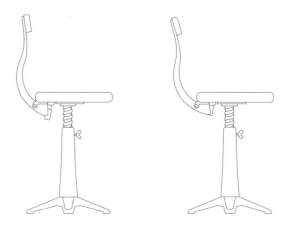

Backrest pivots on armrest, 1958

The backrest pivots backward on ball and socket joints set into rubber flexing mounts, which connect the backrest to the armrest with die-cast aluminium spines. This movement allows a user to recline their back without moving their legs. Although this movement pattern is similar to that of the Unknown chair of 1872, the use of pivoting joints between the armrests and the seat is a unique solution. This design informs the FS Chair of 1980, which employs armrests in the first synchronized movement mechanism.

MAA Chair, p40

Backrest and seat tilt on four pivot points, 1980

The seat and backrest recline on two spring-loaded pivot points under the seat, a pivot point at the junction of the armrest and backrest, and a fourth flexing plastic pivot point at the vertex of the armrest. This is the first movement method that allows the backrest and seat to move simultaneously but at a differing angle (the backrest moves further than the seat as the user leans backward). This is referred to as a 'synchronized' recline. The mechanism allows a user's feet to remain on the ground as the body sinks and reclines from the knees backward, eliminating the sensation of falling out of the chair backward that was common to chairs with a central pivot point. This movement method was emulated by several subsequent chairs designed during the 1980s and early 90s. Although it is rare today that chairs use the armrests as part of the movement mechanism, it is now standard that backrests and seats are able to move independently.

FS Chair, p53

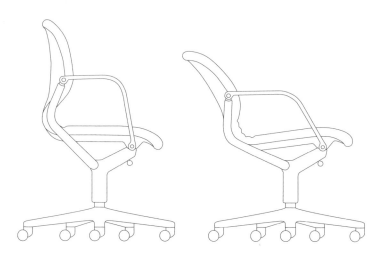

Seat tilts and sinks on front pivot, 1984

The seat sinks and reclines on a spring-loaded pivot point under the front of the seat, while the backrest flexes backward from the seat on bilateral plastic spines. Like the FS Chair of 1980, this movement method allows the backrest and seat to move simultaneously but at differing angles – however, the Equa Chair does so without pivoting joints in the armrests. The angle between the backrest and seat opens as both elements recline, which allows the backrest to recline further than the seat. Because the seat pivots and sinks from its front, the user's feet remain on the ground. The resistance against the recline is controlled with a turning knob that adjusts the tension of the spring-loaded pivot point.

Equa Chair, p57

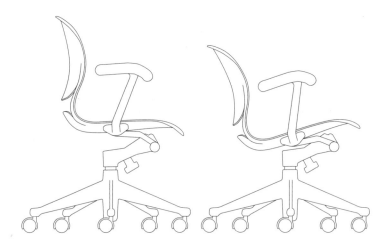

As the sitter leans back, a lever redirects the force of the movement to raise and move the seat forward on four pivoting points: at the arm-rest, the intersection of the backrest and seat, and under the seat. The weight placed on the seat resists this lever and automatically adjusts the stiffness of the recline to the sitter's weight. This movement pattern also opens the angle between the torso and legs as the sitter reclines, which increases blood flow between the upper and lower body. Referred to as a 'teeter-totter' mechanism in the furniture industry, this movement method has been employed by several subsequent chairs and remains common today.

Picto, p58

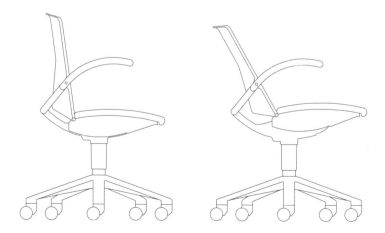

Backrest and seat tilt and sink on four pivot points, 1994

The backrest and seat recline and sink independently of one another on four bars mounted on two spring-loaded pivot points under the front of the seat. The angle between the backrest and the seat can increase by up to 20 degrees as the sitter reclines. Because the pivot points are so far below the seat front, the seated person's entire body pivots backward and sinks from their ankles, while their feet remain on the ground. Resistance against recline is controlled with a turning knob that adjusts the tension of the spring-loaded coils. This movement method has been emulated and modified by countless subsequent chairs and is the most commonly used in new chair designs.

Aeron Chair, p61

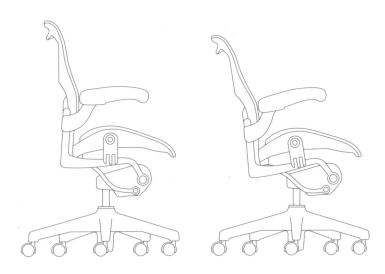

The seat reclines on a spring-loaded pivot point under the front of the seat and the backrest tilts from side to side on two bilateral pivoting joints to the armrests. Because the recline and sideways motion can be engaged independently, or in combination with each other, the user is given an enormous range of freedom. The resistance against recline is adjustable but the resistance against sideways motion is not. While the chairs of the 1980s and 90s moved along a single axis – forward and backward – this movement method allows the body to move relatively unconstrained by a predetermined pattern.

ON, p78

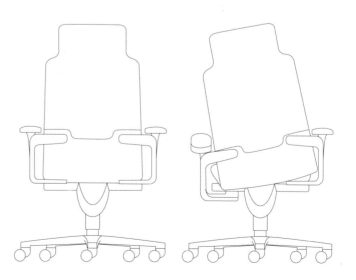

Appendix

Record of Personal Interviews

Emilio Ambasz, Designer, Architect	Bologna	22nd July, 2009
Mario Bellini, Designer	Milan	7th March, 2008
Egon Brüning, Head of Product Development, Vitra	Weil am Rhein	19th October, 2007
Donald Chadwick, Designer	Los Angeles	25th February, 2007
Antonio Citterio, Designer	Milan	6th March, 2007
Niels Diffrient, Designer	Ridgefield, CT	13th February, 2007
William Dowell, Ergonomist, Herman Miller	Holland, MI	28th March, 2008
Tom Eich, Designer, IDEO	New York	20th December, 2007
Fritz Frenkler, Designer, F / P Design	Munich	14th October, 2008
Marianne Goebl, Public Relations Manager, Vitra	Weil am Rhein	19th October, 2007
David Gresham, Designer	New York	20th December, 2007
Harold Gründl, Designer, EOOS	Vienna	9th October, 2008
Gloria Jacobs, Archivist, Herman Miller	Holland, MI	27th March, 2008
Kurt Heidman, Chief Engineer, Steelcase	Caledonia, MI	26th March, 2008
Hitoshi Makino, Designer	Milan	23rd October, 2007
Alberto Meda, Designer	Milan	23rd October, 2007
Jeffrey Osborne	New York	20th December, 2007
Thomas Overthun, Designer, IDEO	San Fransico	20th February, 2008
Jeff Reuschel, Designer, Haworth	Holland, MI	25th March, 2008
Richard Sapper, Designer	Milan	12th March, 2008
Werner Sauer, Designer	Hildesheim	16th October, 2008
Burkhardt Schmitz, Designer, Studio 7.5	Berlin	15th October, 2008
Mark Schurman, Director of Communications, Herman Miller	Holland, MI	27th March, 2008
John Small, Partner, Foster + Partners	Boston	5th December, 2007
Alana Stevens, Senior Marketing Director, Knoll	New York	19th December, 2007
Dr Josef Strasser, Senior Curator, Die Neue Sammlung	Munich	22nd October, 2007
Gareth Williams, Curator	London	16th October, 2007
Carola Zwick, Designer, Studio 7.5	Berlin	15th October, 2008

Bibliography

ISRAEL, FRED, ED. *1897 Sears Roebuck Catalogue.* New York: Chelsea House, 1968. 646.

AMBASZ, EMILIO. *Emilio Ambasz: Natural Architecture and Artificial Design.* Milan: Electa, 2001.

ANDERSSON, GUNNAR, THOMAS W. MCNEILL. *Lumbar Spinal Stenosis.* St. Louis: Mosby-Year, 1992.

ANTONELLI, PAOLA. *Workspheres: Design and Contemporary Work Styles.* New York: Museum of Modern Art, 2001.

ARONSON, JOSEPH. *The Encyclopedia of Furniture.* New York: Crown, 1965. 81.

BAUDRILLARD, JEAN. *The System of Objects.* London: Verso, 1996.

BERRY, JOHN. *Herman Miller: The Purpose of Design.* New York: Rizzoli, 2004.

BRANDES, UTA. *Citizen Office: Ideen und Notizen zu einer Neuen Bürowelt.* Göttingen: Steidl, 1994.

CAPLAN, RALPH. *The Design of Herman Miller.* New York: Whitney Library of Design, 1976.

DARWIN, CHARLES. *The Origin of Species.* London: Penguin Group, 1968.

CRANZ, GALEN. *The Chair: Rethinking Culture, Body, and Design.* New York: W.W. Norton, 1998.

The Design Process at Herman Miller. Minneapolis: Walker Art Center, 1975.

FIELL, CHARLOTTE AND PETER FIELL. *1000 Chairs.* Ed. Simone Philippi, Susanne Uppenbrock. Cologne: Taschen, 2005.

FISCHER, VOLKER, ED. *The Office Swivel Chair by Klaus Franck and Werner Sauer.* Frankfurt: Verlag Form, 1998.

FORTY, ADRIAN. *Objects of Desire: Design and Society, 1750-1980.* London: Thames and Hudson, 1986. 120-155.

GIEDION, SIGFRIED. *Mechanization Takes Command.* New York: Oxford University Press, 1948.

LARRABEE, ERIC AND MASSIMO VIGNELLI. *Knoll Design.* New York: H. N. Abrams, 1981.

LUTZ, BRIAN. *Knoll.* Ed. Dung Ngo. New York: Rizzoli International Publications, 2010.

MÁCEL, OTAKAR. *2100 Metal Tubular Chairs.* Rotterdam: Van Hezik-Fonds 90, 2006.

MEEL, JURIAAN VAN. *The European Office.* Rotterdam: 010, 2000.

NELSON, GEORGE. *George Nelson On Design.* New York: Whitney Library of Design, 1979.

NEUHART, JOHN AND MARILYN NEUHART. *Eames Design: The Work of the Office of Charles and Ray Eames.* New York: H. N. Abrams, 1989.

OPSVIK, PETER. *Rethinking Sitting.* Oslo: Gaidaros Forlag, 2008.

OTTILLINGER, EVA. *Gebrüder Thonet: Möbel Aus Gebogenem Holz.* Vienna: Böhlau, 2003.

PICCHI, FRANCESCA. *Alberto Meda.* Milan: Editrice Abitare Segesta, 2003.

PROPST, ROBERT. *The Office, A Facility Based on Change.* Elmhurst IL: Business, 1968.

RADICE, BARBARA. *Ettore Sottsass: A Critical Biography.* New York: Rizzoli, 1993.

REMMERS, BURKHARD. *Wilkhahn: 100 Years +.* Ludwigsburg: Avedition, 2008.

SCHEPPE, WOLFGANG. *Growing a Chair: Das Büro Und Sein Stuhl: Überlegungen und Entwicklungen Zum Bürostuhl.* Weil am Rhein: Vitra Design Museum, 2004.

SEVEREN, MAARTEN VAN. *Maarten van Severen: Work.* Oostkamp: Stichting Kunstboek, 2004.

SZENASY, SUSAN S. *Office Furniture.* New York: Facts on File, 1984.

TILLEY, ALVIN. *The Measure of Man and Woman: Human Factors in Design.* New York: Wiley, 2002.

VEGESACK, ALEXANDER VON AND JOCHEN EISENBRAND, EDS. *George Nelson: Architect, Writer, Designer, Teacher.* Weil am Rhein: Vitra Design Museum, 2008.

VEGESACK, ALEXANDER VON. *100 Masterpieces from the Vitra Design Museum Collection.* Weil am Rhein: Museum, 1996.

WHITAKER, JOHN O. *National Audubon Society Field Guide to North American Mammals.* New York: Knopf, 1996.

WINDLIN, CORNEL, AND ROLF FEHLBAUM. *Project Vitra: Sites, Products, Authors, Museum, Collections, Signs.* Basel: Birkhäuser, 2008.

WOODSON, WESLEY E., BARRY TILLMAN AND PEGGY TILLMAN. *Human Factors Design Handbook: Information and Guidelines for the Design of Systems, Facilities, Equipment, and Products for Human Use.* New York: McGraw-Hill, 1992.

Index

All reasonable efforts have been made to contact the copyright holders of the photographs used in this book. We apologize to anyone that we have been unable to reach.

Alias: 75 middle
Allseating: 76 middle
Emilio Ambasz: 64 top
Avarte: 48 top
B&B Italia: 74 bottom
Cappellini: 62 bottom
Castelli: 59 top
Nitzan Cohen: 30 top, 30 bottom
De Padova: 59 bottom
Niels Diffrient: 22
Thomas Dix: 55 top
Driade: 63 middle
Marc Eggimann: 62 middle
Emeco: 35 bottom
Bernd Franck: 43 bottom
Freud Museum: 32 top
Giroflex: 70 top
HÅG: 52 bottom, 54 top, 65 bottom, 71 bottom
Hans Hansen: 60 bottom, 64 middle, 67, 74 top, 76 top
Herman Miller: 36 middle, 37, 40 top, 40 bottom, 41 middle, 43 middle, 46 bottom, 47 top, 47 middle, 52 middle, 57, 58 top, 61, 62 top, 64 bottom, 70 middle, 72 middle, 77 bottom, 78 bottom
Hon: 69 top
Humanscale: 65 top, 68 middle, 76 bottom
Itoki: 72 top
Andreas Jung: 34 bottom
Keilhauer: 75 bottom
KI: 52 top
Klöber: 34 middle, 70 bottom
Knoll: 24, 36 top, 42 middle, 42 bottom, 44 middle, 48 middle, 48 bottom, 50 top, 51 top, 51 bottop, 60 middle, 68 bottom, 72 bottom, 79
Daniel Krause: 49, 54 middle
Library of Congress, Prints & Photos Division: 16
A. Laurenzo, Die Neue Sammlung: 30 middle, 32 top, 36 bottom, 41 top, 44 bottom, 43 top, 45, 46 middle, 55 middle

Macatré: 44 top
Material-Environment.com: 42 top
Okamura: 66 bottom
Rohde & Grahl: 69 bottom
Sears Roebuck Catalogue: 31 top
Sedus: 66 top
Sotheby's: 34 bottom
Special Collections Library Wageningen UR: 8
Steelcase: 50 bottom, 55 bottom, 56 bottom, 65 middle, 66 middle, 68 top, 73, 75 top, 77 middle, 78 top
Stoll Giroflex AG: 32 middle
Ezra Stoller / Esto: 18
Studio One: 74 middle
Sunar-Hauserman: 54 bottom
Tecta: 41 bottom
Thonet GmbH: 28 middle, 33
Tom Vack: 77 top
US Patent Office: 14, 28 top, 28 bottom
Vitra: 56 middle, 58 middle, 63 top, 63 bottom
Vitra Design Museum: 29, 31 middle, 31 bottom, 38 middle
Hans J. Wegners Tegnestue: 38 top
Wilkhahn: 46 top, 53, 58 bottom, 60 top, 69 middle, 78 middle
Wright: 35 top, 35 middle, 38 bottom
Yogaback: 59 middle
Nigel Young, Foster + Partners: 56 top
Zoeftig: 50 middle

Benjamin Pardo, Director of Design at Knoll, took an interest in this project from its beginning. I thank Benjamin and Knoll for providing an introduction to dozens of industry experts and for their intellectual, moral and financial support, without which this project would have been impossible.

Without the designers, engineers, company representatives, archivists and curators who offered me their knowledge of office chair design, this book's content would be largely superficial and imprecise.

Over the four years it took to complete this book, a number of curious and dedicated designers helped make this project a reality. Laura Settino was instrumental in the research and classification of the hundreds of chairs that were examined in the making of this book. Allon Kapeller-Lieberman, Evangelina La, Panna Sethvarankul, Madison Watson, and Chaichen Wu spent long and silent hours gathering information and producing illustrations.

Nathan Antolik was involved in this project from the beginning as a designer, editor and critic. My gratitude goes to him for his patience and persistence.

Phaidon Press Limited
Regent's Wharf
All Saints Street
London N1 9PA

Phaidon Press Inc.
180 Varick Street
New York, NY 10014

www.phaidon.com

First published 2011
© 2011 Phaidon Press Limited

ISBN 978 0 7148 6103 6

A CIP catalogue record for this book is available from the British Library.

Edited and designed by Nathan Antolik
Printed in China